PRAISE FOR
THE TOP 12 RESOURCES

Jonathan's heart for the volunteer youth worker shines through in this very helpful and very practical book. The ideas and concepts that Jonathan provides are the kind that you can use right away in your own youth ministry setting.

> Dave Ambrose
> Youth and Outreach Pastor, Oak Hills
> Church
> The CORE Training Team, Youth
> Specialties

For years Jonathan McKee has been providing a dynamite (FREE!) resource for youth workers through his website (www.thesourceforyouthministry.com). Now you can get the best of his thinking in a single volume. It is handy, easy to read and very practical. But don't let any of that fool you—it is also sharp, poignant and real. I have been teaching and leading youth ministry for decades, and this is the best single volume on pragmatic programming I have ever seen. This is a must on every youth worker's shelf!

> Chap Clark
> Associate Professor of Youth, Family
> and Culture
> Fuller Theological Seminary

To say this book is practical would be an understatement. From cover to cover you'll find tips, tricks, ideas and resources that will strengthen your ministry to students. This book is one that you will reach for over and over again as you strive to build an effective youth ministry.

Kurt Johnston
Junior High Pastor, Saddleback Church
Mission Viejo, California
Author, *Controlled Chaos: Making Sense of Junior High Ministry*

I'll be honest: Most of the game books I go through I can't use, or I have to spend half of the time rewriting stuff to fit my kids—but I like reading Jonathan. He talks to you on a level you can understand and he gives you the stuff that you can use THAT WORKS. When you read this, you'll find yourself taking notes, marking pages and planning out your entire year with stuff that youth ministers are starving for: GREAT IDEAS!

Fred Lynch
Director of Urban Ministries
Josh McDowell Ministry

Jonathan McKee is one of the most creative and innovative youth leaders that I know. His new book will do more than simply give you fun ideas to use with your group; it will provide the foundation for many discussions on the issues of life. I wish that I had this resource back when I worked with teens. Not only does he provide details for working with kids, but he also provides details for working with "big church" leadership.

Al Menconi
President
Al Menconi Ministries

It's a WOW! Nitty-gritty-day-in-day-out practical! *The Top 12 Resources Youth Workers Want* will get you through dry spells, provide you with tons of easy-to-use tools and prepare you for more than a year of great ministry. Reading this book reminded me of one of the reasons I love youth ministry—it's just plain fun!

> Jenny Morgan
> National Training Director
> Youth for Christ/USA

The Top 12 Resources Youth Workers Want is an entirely different kind of youth ministry book. It's fresh, exciting, extremely useful and completely filled with great ideas you can use every week!

> Bill Muir
> Vice President
> Youth for Christ/USA

For the last few years I've been recommending Jonathan's resource website to youth workers around the country. This book will be a tremendous asset to anyone who has to lead a game, run a program or come up with something meaningful and fun (in the next five minutes) for a roomful of teenagers. And what youth worker doesn't need that?

> Laurie Polich
> Author, *Help! I'm a Small-Group Leader!*

If you're just looking for another book on youth ministry philosophy, I suggest you look elsewhere. But if you want some practical ideas to help make your next youth meeting or activity really sizzle, I suggest you look no further than this book! My friend Jon McKee has been doing youth ministry long enough to know that even when you have a great philosophy, you still need to know what to do (and what not to do) when the kids show up. This book will not only give you the practical help you need, but it will also renew your confidence and enthusiasm for youth ministry. I highly recommend this book!

> Wayne Rice
> Cofounder, Youth Specialties
> Executive Director, Understanding
>   Your Teenager

Jonathan McKee knows youth ministry! As a youth worker and veteran Youth for Christ staff member, he's known for pulling together great ideas for games, planning, teaching, small groups and recruiting staff and especially for sharing these resources with others. Jonathan's book is an excellent compilation of many of these youth ministry classics—plus his own fresh and straightforward advice and expertise. It's a must-have tool for all youth workers to read and then keep within reach!

> Mike Work
> National Director, DCLA Ministries
> Youth for Christ/USA

Jonathan R. McKee
Creator of www.thesourceforyouthministry.com

the Top 12 Resources Youth Workers Want

Gospel Light

PUBLISHING STAFF
William T. Greig, Chairman
Kyle Duncan, Publisher
Dr. Elmer L. Towns, Senior Consulting Publisher
Pam Weston, Senior Editor
Patti Pennington Virtue, Associate Editor
Jeff Kempton, Editorial Assistant
Bayard Taylor, M.Div., Senior Editor, Biblical and Theological Issues
Kevin Parks, Cover Designer
Rosanne Richardson, Cover Production
Debi Thayer, Designer

Library of Congress Cataloging-in-Publication Data
McKee, Jonathan, 1970-
    The top 12 resources youth workers want : offline one-stop shop for
    youth ministry / Jonathan McKee.
        p. cm.
Includes bibliographical references.
    ISBN 0-8307-3062-1 (pbk.)
    1. Church work with youth. I. Title: Top twelve resources youth
    workers want. II. Title.
    BV4447 .M24 2002
    259'.23—dc21   2002005383

2 3 4 5 6 7 8 9 10 / 09 08 07 06 05 04

MANY THANKS!

I would like to thank Youth For Christ, especially Gary Fox, for believing in me and giving me a start in full-time youth ministry.

Thank you Jim Burns for helping out the little guy. You care about the youth worker more than anyone I know. It's nice to know someone so real. Thanks for helping me through this whole process.

Thanks to Teddi Pettee and Dave Ambrose for helping me work and rework this book.

Thanks to Leonard Lee who taught me the basics—many of which are reflected in this book.

Thanks to my dad, Tom McKee, Sr., an old-school youth worker, who has helped me since "the beginning" (not Genesis 1:1—he's not *that* old!).

But most of the thanks go to my wife. Lori, you are not only the best proof-reader I know (she missed her calling as an editor), but you are also my love and my joy. Thanks for putting up with me!

Jonathan

CONTENTS

FOREWORD

A few years ago I was speaking in South Africa and a couple of key youth ministry leaders in that country took me to lunch. Their agenda was to complain about the way we in the United States were using, or rather *not* using, our websites. Their need was leadership ideas and resources. Because of the cost of publishing books and the economy in most parts of the world, the Web can become a wonderful place to offer free resources and leadership ideas. Although things are rapidly changing now, the only person I knew of at the time who was doing an effective job of offering great resources free of charge was Jonathan McKee.

Almost every week I find myself looking forward to reading Jonathan's latest e-mail newsletter, the "Resource Ezine" from *The Source for Youth Ministry*. I love it. The material is always practical and usually a bit goofy, with articles such as "Another Successful Use of Duct Tape." As you read through this book you will definitely feel as though you've gained a new friend in Jonathan McKee. As a youth worker and communicator *par excellence*, Jonathan is just like his book—practical, funny and helpful *and* he knows what he is talking about!

When I first started to read *The Top 12 Resources Youth Workers Want*, I thought it was more of a fun-and-games book. While it certainly has that element to it, it also has incredibly practical ideas about some of the very important ingredients for effective ministry with students. I would pay the price of this book just for the sections on student leadership and small groups.

As you begin to use this book, you will become a part of an ever-growing community of youth workers around the world who regularly look to Jonathan's leadership for resources in youth ministry. (You can join that growing community at *The Source for Youth Ministry* by logging onto www.thesourcefym.com.)

I have often heard it said that "the essence of creativity is the ability to copy." I usually quote that statement with a smile, but it's true. One of the most important decisions you can ever make to influence and impact students is to build a great resource library. With the use of the right resources, you can be freed up to spend more time in ministry and in relationship with kids. I love 1 Thessalonians 2:8:

> We loved you so much that we were delighted to share with you not only the gospel of God but our lives as well, because you had become so dear to us.

With that Scripture in mind, we realize that while the call of Christ is to present the gospel, we can do that best by building relationships. Equipped with your Bible and *The Top 12 Resources Youth Workers Want* and a deep desire to spend time with kids, you *can* make an eternal difference.

Jim Burns
President, YouthBuilders
YouthBuilders.com

What's the Trick to Leading Games?

THE SEVEN DEADLY SINS OF GAME LEADING

The scene: Wednesday night. 7:00 P.M. Youth group. Solid attendance, positive attitudes—and then, it's game time! **Enter stage left:** Youth ministry intern, embarrassed, announces, "OK! Now we're going to play a game!"

A few audible groans resound throughout the room. As the intern searches for supplies and scurries around the stage trying to find the props, conversations resume around the room. Trying to reclaim control of her audience, the intern raises her voice—and completely loses the group. Sound familiar? We've all seen it happen!

Well, if you're going to mess up, you might as well mess up bad! Do any of the Seven, and you can chase students away rather than bring them in.

THE SEVEN DEADLY SINS OF GAME LEADING

DEADLY SIN NUMBER ONE

Tell the crowd that you're going to play a game!

The best way to ruin a game is to tell kids that you're going to play one! Youth groups across the nation consistently use this pathetic transition: "Okay, we're going to play a mixer now!" But does the average junior higher off the street know what a mixer is? Yeah! It's the thing you use to stir cake mix!

> **Just start the game— you don't need permission. Ten minutes later kids will be looking at each other saying, "Hey, we're playing games!"**

In the early '90s I started a campus outreach for a group of unchurched junior high students. The first week about 12 of them showed up to my house for *free* root beer floats. They didn't know what was going on—all they knew is that their friend told them to come to this fun thing with *free* root beer floats! They weren't expecting games; most unchurched students aren't used to playing them.

When they got there I told them, "Hey, thanks for coming. Tonight we're going to have *free root beer floats*! Who thinks they can drink more than two? How about three? Four? All right, we're going to have the floats in a minute, but first . . . get into two lines. Now I want to see which line has the best reflexes."

Notice what I did. I didn't break rule number one of The Seven. I didn't tell them we were going to play a game. For this group it was crucial. These are the kinds of kids that if you said, "Come on in! We're going to play some *games*," they would have thought I was the clown that Mom rented for their tenth birthday party.

Before the kids knew it they were playing the game. As a matter of fact, they forgot all about the floats and were focused on trying to beat the other team.

When starting a game, just start doing it. For example: "Hey, before we get started today I want everyone on this side of the room to scoot one foot that way while my staff runs this rope between you."

My friend Phil ran a ministry that reached a tough group of students. So did my friend Lee. Phil always complained that he had trouble finding stuff to do: "My kids don't like games!" He spent two frustrating years programming his weekly outreach without any games at all. However, Lee worked with a much tougher group and he played games all the time. The difference was he never told them they were going to play one. He would just pull out a raw fish, a pillow and a blindfold and say, "I need a volunteer!" I've never seen so many kids with nothing in common have so much fun together. I'd always hear Lee's kids say, "Man, Lee always gets us to do the craziest stuff!"

Just start the game—you don't need permission. Ten minutes later kids will be looking at each other saying, "Hey, we're playing games!"

DEADLY SIN NUMBER TWO

Wing it.

That's right—if you really want to chase students away, *don't be prepared!* Just whip up a game a few minutes before a program and figure out what you need later.

The truth is, time is always crucial because attention spans are short. In this fast-food-microwave-quick-cut-MTV-Minute-Rice-Taco-Bell-drive-thru generation, kids are used to having what they want stimulating their eyes, ears and mouth *every second*. If you're going to lead a game that requires everyone to have a balloon and piece of string, make sure you have multiple staff members ready to hand out balloons. Also have the strings precut and several staff members ready to hand them out.

I once witnessed an intern who thought that he didn't need to plan ahead for his campus outreach program. He would look up a few games on my website a half hour before his program and pick up the supplies on the way to the meeting. Every week he was late because he never found what he needed at a single store and so had to make multiple stops. Even if he did buy everything, he wouldn't have it laid out, prepared and ready to go.

I'll never forget the time that he chose a game that required two marshmallows with a piece of string tied around them. He brought two kids up front and then ran to his grocery bag to pull out a bag of unopened marsh-mallows and a new roll of string. He tore open the marshmallows and handed each of the kids one. Then he tried to open the string. At first he couldn't get the plastic off. Finally, when he managed to get the covering off, he discovered that he didn't have anything to cut the string with.

Within a minute the kids weren't paying attention. They were talking with each other, throwing things and generally beginning to look for trouble. Meanwhile, my intern started biting the string, pulling it and trying everything he could to cut it. He finally asked if anyone in the audience had something to cut string with. By this time several other staff members had come up front to try to help him. After the string was cut, while he and the staff were trying to tie the string to the marshmallows, a fight broke out in the bleachers.

I don't think they ever actually played the game that day. They did have to write an incident report to the vice principal, however, explaining why there was a fight at this campus outreach event.

Have *everything* ready. And if you've never done a particular game before, test it! You can test it on your staff at a staff meeting or on a small group of leadership students that are kind and forgiving (let me know if you meet any!). So many times I thought I was the Game Master, and all of a sudden I'm coming up short in front of a bunch of kids with a game that doesn't work. Not a pretty sight. Test it! Test it! Test it!

DEADLY SIN NUMBER THREE

Use *chaperones*, not *youth workers*.

If you want to mess up great opportunities for your staff, don't have them playing the games with the kids. Just have them stand around the edges

> **Game time is the perfect opportunity for the staff to break the ice with students.**

with their arms crossed yelling out, "Stop that!" or "You quiet down!" every once in awhile. This not only damages the enthusiasm and energy in your group, but it is also a disservice to your students and staff. Through the years, staff and students playing together has proven to be a major relationship builder.

Hopefully your staff members are trained to hang out with kids, not merely to chaperone. Mere chaperones are no fun, and most students don't want a relationship with one. Staff members can, and should, be so much more than that. They should be participating purposefully in all your events and hanging out with kids any chance they get. They should laugh with them, talk with them, cry with them—whatever it takes. Game time is the perfect opportunity for the staff to break the ice with students.

I love it when one of my volunteers runs games and allows me a chance to play! Once I played a game where we were divided into two teams and were given Q-tips and straws. Several people on each team had to balance paper cups on the tops of their heads while the rest of the team protected them while attacking the other teams. When my staff guy said "Go," I got a bunch of the junior high guys and told them we should all attack a girl named Tonya on the other team. All of us bombarded her with Q-tips until her cup finally fell off her head. Students reminded me for years about the time we annihilated Tonya with Q-tips. Fun memories make lasting impressions.

Games are great times to bond with students. Don't miss this opportunity!

DEADLY SIN NUMBER FOUR

Explain the game for more than 30 seconds.

As we all know, time and attention spans are short. Part of being prepared for a game is knowing how to explain it quickly. Give the basics—maybe with a visual example—and jump straight into "Ready, set, go!" Giving highly detailed explanations will only serve to confuse or bore kids.

Don't be afraid to start a game even when some are still confused. Staff members can help push these people along once you start.

DEADLY SIN NUMBER FIVE

Take tons of time to divide teams.

Same principle as number four: If you spend all kinds of time dividing teams, students will lose interest before the game's even started. Then you have to crawl out of a hole!

Have a plan to divide teams quickly. Always try to use natural divisions: grade levels, gender, half of the room, etc. Only number off as a last resort!

We used to play good ol' fashioned dodgeball at youth group. At first we tried to number students off, making the teams completely even. We'd get halfway through numbering them and some students were switching, even leaving the line up. Many lost interest before the game began. I finally learned to say, "Seventh graders over here and eighth graders over there!" If there were way more eighth graders than seventh, I would yell, "All staff play with the seventh graders." This always upped the level of competition.

Whatever you do, *have a plan*. Do it swiftly and clearly. The speed with which you do it may be more important than having the exact number on each team.

DEADLY SIN NUMBER SIX

Let *any* volunteer lead games.

As you can see from the first five sins of game leading, not *every* staff member is cut out to be the up-front guy or gal. The game leader must be trained in dynamic, enthusiastic communication. He or she must be equipped with resources and given an opportunity to lead a game in a staff meeting or in an occasional youth group. If you're like me, you value your staff as much as you value your life. Don't tie meat around the necks of your volunteers and then throw them to the lions. Teach them. Show them. Give them a chance to rehearse and evaluate.

We can be honest. Some people just aren't gifted at being up front. Don't use these people to lead games. A key to a successful program is putting staff in roles in which they are gifted and feel comfortable. This isn't harsh—this is good leadership. If you help volunteers find their gifts and give them the opportunity to use them, you'll have a happier—and more effective—staff team.

By the way, if something goes wrong, play it off. Games will go sour—it's a fact. When they do, use the opportunity to make fun of it. If a game goes wrong and the leader is funny about it, kids will still have a good time and relationships will still be strengthened—after all, that's the point, right?

DEADLY SIN NUMBER SEVEN

Make sure the audience can't see the action.

The last way to guarantee messing up your game plan is to make sure that the audience can't see what's happening. This is most common with up-front games like the ones described in chapter 2. These are games where students are up front doing something while the audience participates by cheering them on. You can guarantee that these kinds of games will be a dud when the audience can't see the action.

"Of course!" you say. But I can't tell you how many times I have seen some cool crowd breaker or up-front game in which a kid is getting doused with syrup or a girl is about to suck a jelly bean out of some Jell-O and I couldn't see because the game leader was standing right in the way! If you're leading a game, *step aside*! Remember, as fun as it is for the game leader to watch, that's not the reason the game is being played. Let the audience see.

Sometimes the room you are meeting in isn't very up-front-game compatible. A common setting for this occurrence is when you have a room where the audience is on the same physical level as the onstage action. Very often when the action starts taking place, the front row will stand up to see better, and then everyone else can't see. Here are a few suggestions to improve the view for your audience:

- Use a makeshift stage. If you don't have one, make one. If you can't make one, then stand people up, put them on chairs or have them lie on tables instead of the ground. Do what it takes so everyone can see.
- Keep everyone seated. If you violate the first of these points and have someone lie on the ground to have eggs dropped in his mouth, it will be hard to keep people in the audience from standing. So follow the first suggestion and your audience will be more likely to listen to you when you ask them to stay seated.
- Use a video feed. Videotape the action up front and project it to a big screen that everyone can see. This will please most crowds.

If you lose the audience during games, you may create a momentum that loses 'em for the whole night. The participation of the whole group is crucial. Utilize staff members to keep energy high and *the audience seated*!

What Are the Best Up-Front Games?

GAMES THAT GRAB ATTENTION AND ENTERTAIN THE GROUP

First allow me to define "up-front" games. These games differ from "all-play" games (check out chapter 3 for those) in that they focus attention on a few students in front of the group or in a staged setting, and the remaining students participate as an audience, cheering for a specific individual or team. All-play games require the active involvement of all students and staff.

So let's not waste time—here are some great up-front games that are very effective and can be used weekly!

THE BEST UP-FRONT GAMES

HAPPY SHAKE

There's nothing like starting youth group off with a grotesque up-front game that makes people howl with laughter. File this one under the fun-with-a-blender category.

Here's what you'll need:

❏ A blender
❏ Several McDonald's Happy Meals

❏ Large clear plastic cups
❏ A big trash can (or two!)

Go to the local McDonald's and pick up three or four Happy Meals. Prepick three or four willing contestants and bring them up front. Make sure you avoid the Seven Deadly Sins of Game Leading—especially numbers two (Wing it) and seven (Make sure the audience can't see the action).

Blend the Happy Meals together (yes, burger, fries *and* drink!) in front of the students; then fill up *clear* cups with an equal amount of the shake for each person. The rest is a race to see who can drink their Happy Shake the fastest. Be careful—you might want one or two big trash cans near the front for participants who don't like the shakes.

COMMIT

I had about 1,400 junior high students and staff crowded into a sanctuary, and we had to keep them entertained before the speaker began. What would you do? Well, it's a sure bet that everyone loves to see someone else get messy, so I went for the ol' pie-in-the-face scenario in a game I call Commit.

Here's what you'll need:

❏ A plastic tarp for the stage area
❏ Pie tins
❏ Whipped cream
❏ Prepared questions (with appropriate pause points to sucker kids in!)

❏ Five really cool prizes
❏ Two assistants
❏ Towels for cleaning up contestants

Commit is a simple game. Explain that you will be asking some questions of the audience. If someone knows the answer to the question, they simply raise their hand *if* they are willing to commit to the consequences of their answer. Then display the prizes that you are offering that evening. (I usually choose something like a Walkman, a bucket of Red Vines—that's red licorice for those of you who are deprived of these because you're not from the West—and a popular basketball jersey. Pick some prizes kids actually want.) Then let them know that if they don't answer the question correctly, they'll be held by your assistant while you smush a pie in their face.

Start the game with a simple question, saying something like: **Question number one.** (Stop here and issue a final warning that anyone who raises their hand is committing to the consequences of their answer if it's wrong!) **OK, here we go: A white liquid that we drink and put on our breakfast cereal that comes from cows is called what?** Hands will shoot up all over the room. Bring one of the volunteers up and have one of your staff members hold them with their arms behind their back. Ask them a bunch of simple questions—their name, what school they go to, etc.; then repeat the actual game question and tell them they have five seconds to answer. Most likely, the student will give the right answer. Award the prize and lead the audience in applause as the contestant returns to their seat. (Be warned, though; some smart-aleck might *want* a pie in his face—I say "his" because it's usually going to be a guy—and purposely say the wrong answer or not answer within the five seconds. Be sure to nail him with the pie the second his time is up or the second he says the wrong answer and escort him off the stage without his prize. Then let everyone know the answer is "milk.")

Now you've got the attention of every kid in the place; they can *taste* the next prize. Here's how I might say the next question: **Question two: In the movie *The Lion King*, the name of the young lion was. . . .** Pause here and hands will fly up everywhere (if they aren't already up). At this point bring up one of the students and ask their name, school, etc. Remind them that they are committed to answer the question correctly or they'll get a pie in their face. Then continue: **Now let me finish the question. In the movie *The Lion King*, the name of the young lion was Simba. Simba's adolescent voice was played by the actor Matthew Broderick. Name**

Matthew's first eight theatrical release films! As you can see, odds are that this kid is gonna get a pie. But if for some reason you have a huge Matthew Broderick fan in the room, the correct answer in chronological order, starting in 1983, is *War Games, Max Dugan Returns, Ladyhawke, 1918, Ferris Bueller's Day Off, On Valentine's Day, Project X* and *Courtship*.

Continue the game in this fashion. I usually throw in some easy questions and then a hard one, in no particular order. Great fun and worth a lot of laughs!

FUNNEL PENNY GAG

This is an age-old game that was passed down to me by my friend Leonard, who had had it passed down to him by another longtime youth worker. Never dismiss a game just because it's been around awhile. What may be old to you could be new to your students!

Here's what you'll need:

❑ A funnel (with a large opening for good water flow!)
❑ Lots of pennies
❑ A glass of ice water
❑ Prizes

Take a funnel and shove the small end down the front of your pants so the wide end is facing up. Put your head back, place a penny on your forehead and close your eyes. Tilt your head forward, dropping the penny off of your forehead and into the funnel. Issue a challenge to students that no one can do what you just did three times in a row.

Bring willing students up and let them try one at a time. It's very simple; most kids will be able to do it fairly easily. Give each kid a prize regardless of how many times they get it in.

Now explain that this is too easy. Tell them you're going to make it harder now and that you're going to try it again, closing your eyes for at least three seconds before dropping the penny in. Once you've proven it can be done, ask who wants to try it. Pick the kid who's the most eager to prove you wrong. Set the volunteer up for the trick and emphasize that they must close their eyes for at least three seconds before dropping the penny in. Let them drop the first two pennies in; then while their eyes are closed for the third try, pour a huge glass of ice water down the funnel! CAUTION: *As always, use caution when choosing your victim—er, volunteer. Some students are embarrassed more easily than others.*

ICE CHEST

This is one of the great up-front games where you give a chance for men to be men—and for them to end up wondering if volunteering was such a good idea!

Here's what you'll need:

- ❏ 20 pounds of ice (or more) per contestant
- ❏ Cooler for each contestant
- ❏ Three scoops (or large plastic cups will also work)
- ❏ Three XXXL T-shirts

Prearrange for three to five guys to come up front and prove how manly they are and for three girls to act as assistants for each guy (that's nine girls, in case you don't feel like doing the math!). Provide each guy with one of the XXXL T-shirts and instruct them to take off their regular shirts (and undershirts) and put on the jumbo ones, making sure to tuck them in *really* well. **Note:** It's a good idea to have the guys remove their shirts and change into the T-shirts prior to the contest.

Have each of the guys stand by a cooler of ice (at least 20 pounds per cooler—I've used about 40) and give each of the girls a large scooper. When you say "Go!" the girls will begin shoveling the ice into their guys' T-shirts. This is hilarious to watch and painful to experience.

Give the 10-second warning after a minute or two, depending on the crowd's interest. You can simply declare the guy with the most ice in his shirt the winner, or you can have the crowd vote by applause. **Hint:** Save yourself a lot of cleanup by having the ice-stuffed guys escorted outside for emptying and changing of clothes.

SODA SLAM

It's always good to have a few games that take little or no preparation, and this game is a cinch. Bring up a few contestants, give them each a soda and tell them the first one to empty their can wins. **Option:** Have them belch when they're done to complete the contest.

Here's what you'll need:

❑ A can of soda for each contestant
❑ A plastic tarp (or plan to do this outside)
❑ A pen for each contestant

You say you've done that before? Okay, try this! Have each contestant turn their can upside down before opening. Take a pen and poke a hole in the bottom sidewall of the can. Have them place their mouths around their can's hole, tilt the can upright and open the top at the same time. All of the soda will flow into their mouths in less than 10 seconds—it's very hard to keep from spitting it out!

SURGICAL GLOVE BLOWUP

If you haven't seen Howie Mandell do this, you're missing out.

Here's what you'll need:

❑ Several pairs of rubber surgical gloves

Have several volunteers come up. Instruct them to pull the gloves over their own heads, all the way down to just above their mouths. Have them blow with their noses, inflating the gloves on their heads. After 90 seconds, see who's blown the largest glove balloon. (Take caution that the balloons don't pop or snap students in the eye!)

TO TELL THE TRUTH

This is just like the TV game show. Beforehand, pick four contestants and take them aside. Ask them to tell you a true funny or interesting story about something that happened to them when they were young, but it has to be a story that can be told in *one sentence* (e.g., "My name is Billy and when I was five, I was walking with my mom and a big guy ran by and grabbed my mom's purse!"). Pick the story that sounds the best and have all four contestants memorize the sentence, replacing the name with their real names (e.g., "My name is Teresa and when I was five, I was walking with my mom and a big guy ran by and grabbed my mom's purse!").

Bring the contestants forward and explain to the audience that although each of them claims the story they tell is theirs, only one of them is telling the truth. Invite the audience to question the contestants (like the old TV show *To Tell the Truth*). Three of the contestants will have to lie through their teeth. Then have the audience vote who they think is telling the truth. Finally, have the person who told the truth step forward. Great fun!

JELL-O SUCK

Easy as it sounds.

Here's what you need:

- ❑ A bowl of Jell-O for each contestant
- ❑ A drinking straw for each contestant (optional)

Ask for volunteers to come forward. You can give them each a straw or just have them put their hands behind their back and bury their faces in the bowls. First one to eat all their Jell-O wins!

JOUST

Why is it that we enjoy beating the snot out of one another? Just a thought!

Here's what you'll need:

- ❑ Two five-gallon buckets
- ❑ Two jousting sticks (4-foot sticks with foam rubber ends) or two pillows
- ❑ Soft area to play (grass area or padded floor)

Place the two buckets upside down, about three feet apart. Have two players stand on the buckets, each with a jousting stick or pillow (pillow-fight style). When you say "Go," each player will try to knock the other player off of their bucket. Try to discourage head shots and other cheap shots. Remember to stop this game while they still want more!

WOOD CHIPPER BLEND

Fresno Youth for Christ gets the Creative Game Award for this one.

If you have a big audience and the capability to project video onto a big screen, this is a great game. Have your live video feed from the parking lot. Pan your outside camera to a wood chipper in the parking lot with all kinds of food next to it. (You could just do this event in a parking lot around a wood chipper, but the video feed to the meeting room is a nice touch.)

Most experienced youth workers only need to hear the words "wood chipper," and they begin to think of 100 ideas of what they could do with one. I had to admit I had never thought of using one before, but the possibilities are endless!

Fresno YFC played a game called "You Pick It, We Chip It." I never quite figured out what the title had to do with the game, but the kids didn't care. The staff brought kids in front of the audience, put them in some protective rain gear and sent them outside to the wood chipper. The audience watched them exit the side door where the video feed immediately picked them up. The object was to see who could get the messiest.

Here's what you'll need:

❏ A wood chipper
❏ Tons of food to be chipped*
❏ Video feed to big screen

❏ Protective rain gear
❏ Plastic safety goggles
❏ Towels for cleaning up contestants

The staff placed the contestants in front of the chipper, a few at a time, and began throwing items in the chipper, which in turn sprayed them all over the contestants. The leaders used eggs, watermelon, lettuce and other messy items (no live animals—or dead ones either!). The one thing I noticed is the obvious fact that the more stuff you have to shred, the better the show! The kids loved it, and I'm sure the youth network in Fresno would say that the event was a success.

> **Simple Live Video-Feed Hookup:** Kids love to see themselves and their friends on the big screen. You can set one up very simply. We went to Radio Shack and bought a couple hundred feet of coaxial cable. We put an RCA jack on each end (converting it to an RCA cable) and plugged one end to a video camera's VIDEO OUT and the other end to a VCR's VIDEO IN. It's as simple as it sounds. Have the VCR go into your TV or VPU, and you've got video. **Note:** You'll still need a wireless mike hooked to your sound system for audio.

* Stop by your local grocer and ask the manager to donate some food that is ready to be pulled off the shelf because the freshness date has expired (but make sure it's not spoiled).

BOBBING FOR BANANAS

Talking about using live video feed reminds me of another fun game I did. In fact, it was my first live video feed. I was in high school at the time, and I helped run a junior high event where we introduced Bobbing for Bananas! This doesn't sound like a big deal unless you're in a church with a baptistry that you've filled with milk, and the bananas are sunk at the bottom four feet down! (Not a smart move—I was young and crazy at the time.) We had a camera at the entrance to the baptistry, interviewing each bobber as they disappeared into the 50-gallon tank for what seemed like minutes before emerging with a banana in their mouth.

Here's what you'll need:

- ❑ Several huge boxes of powdered milk
- ❑ Large swimming area that can hold milk—baptistry *not* recommended!
- ❑ Approximately 20 peeled bananas
- ❑ Bucket (for soggy bananas)
- ❑ Towels for wet bobbers
- ❑ Live video feed (optional)

CANDLE BLOW/GINGER ALE DRINK

Here's what you'll need:

- ❑ Small table and chairs
- ❑ Two lighters
- ❑ Two candles with sturdy holders—no need to burn contestants!
- ❑ Two clear glasses
- ❑ A bottle of ginger ale

Here's how this one works: Two people sit very close at a small table in chairs facing each other, and they compete to drink a full glass of ginger ale. Each contestant has a candle (which they must hold at all times) in their left hand resting on the left corner of the table, a lighter and a glass or can of ginger ale in front of them. They may only drink the ginger ale when the candle is lit. Each tries to blow out the other person's candle while trying to finish their own drink first. The winner is the person who can finish the ginger ale first with their candle still lit.

Rules for players:

- If you move your candle off the left side of the table, you lose!
- If you touch the other person's candle, you lose!
- If you touch the other person's ginger ale, you lose!
- If you touch the other person's lighter, you lose!
- You must find the balance between drinking and blowing out your opponent's candle.

CLOTHESPINS ON FACE

This one's easy. Here's what you'll need:

- ❑ About 200 clothespins

Bring four students up front, each with a partner and a pile of 50 or so clothespins in front of them. Their partners have 90 seconds to put clothespins all over their faces. No hair—just face, eyebrows, ears, lips, nose, etc. The one with the most clothespins at the end of the designated time is the winner.

WHEEL O' DOOM

Students always love prizes. And students always love our Wheel o' Doom as a way to win a prize.

Here's what you'll need for the Wheel o' Doom:

- ❑ Two 2x4 pieces of lumber 5- to 6-feet long (one for the stand and one to hold the wheel)
- ❑ A 2-foot in diameter circular piece of 1/4-inch plywood
- ❑ A large bolt
- ❑ A wrench (to fit the bolt)
- ❑ A hammer
- ❑ A saw
- ❑ Nails

Build a Wheel o' Doom using one 2x4 for the stand and one for the pole. Attach the round piece of wood on a large bolt at the top of the 2x4, so it can spin freely. Leave a little bit of the pole above the top of the circle so that you can attach a pointer made from cardboard or plastic. Basically it is a homemade Wheel of Fortune. There is enough room on the circle to tape eight pie-shaped paper pieces with different descriptions of activities printed on them. Spin the wheel and the pointer will point to a given pie piece when the wheel stops spinning.

Here's what you'll need to play:

- ❑ Baby bottles
- ❑ Soda
- ❑ Baby food
- ❑ Snow trip certificates
- ❑ Saltine crackers
- ❑ Prizes for winners
- ❑ Eggs
- ❑ Spam
- ❑ Hot peppers
- ❑ Whistles
- ❑ Certificates for fast food with staff

You can use the Wheel o' Doom many different ways. At outreach events, we put all the Basic Info Cards (the cards students filled out on the way in; see p. 205 for a sample) into a bucket and draw out two at a time for Wheel o' Doom competitions. We bring two contestants up and have them spin the wheel. They either do that activity or just win that prize! This game is great fun and a great way to make students really earn prizes!

The following sample choices give you an idea of activities you can use for the pie pieces. These can vary—just use your creativity! As you can see, we use this as an opportunity to give away some cool stuff.

- Baby Bottle Suck
- Raw Egg
- Baby Food
- Coke Chug

- Spam for Snow Trip
- Hot Pepper
- Cracker Whistle
- Fast Food with Staff

Clear as mud? OK, here's what these activities are:

Baby Bottle Suck: Each contestant sucks a baby bottle full of cola. The one who finishes first gets a cool prize.

Raw Egg: Each contestant chooses a partner. One of the partners lays down while the other extends their arms straight out, cracks an egg and drops it into their partner's mouth. The winning twosome gets a cool prize.

Baby Food: The first contestant to eat an entire jar of baby food wins a cool prize. (The grosser the food choice, the better!)

Coke Chug: Contestants race to see who can swig Coke the fastest. The winner gets a cool prize.

Spam for Snow Trip: The first contestant to eat a can of Spam wins a certificate to attend our Snow Trip (or any other special event) for free.

Hot Pepper: Contestants race to eat a hot pepper the fastest. (Be careful not to make it too hot; some peppers can hurt a student). The winner gets a cool prize.

Cracker Whistle: The first person to eat a saltine cracker and whistle wins a cool prize.

Fast Food with Staff: Two students each get a certificate for FREE fast food with a staff person. No contest required!

What Are the Best All-Play Games?

GAMES THAT GET EVERYONE MOVING

Let's face it, some games are DUDS! Each of us has probably made that regretful purchase of a game book in some Christian bookstore or off some website and found only two games that are actually good ones. The rest are feeble attempts to print something different, rather than concentrating on what works!

Let's not waste time. Here are some proven games that, whether you have played them already or not, still work!

THE BEST ALL-PLAY GAMES

GRAB IT

I have a special place in my heart for this game, because it was introduced to me by a close friend and mentor who helped me get started in ministry years ago. When I started a campus outreach in 1993, this was the first game I played. (I'm wiping a sentimental tear from my eye.)

Here's what you'll need:

- ❑ Two buckets full of water
- ❑ Two plastic tarps
- ❑ Two bars of soap
- ❑ Towels
- ❑ A quarter

Divide the group into two teams, placing each team in a line, single file, and leaving about three feet between the teams. Instruct all team members to sit down and hold hands. Put a bar of soap in a bucket of water and place it at the back of the line between the two teams. If you're playing indoors on carpet, protect it with a layer of towels or a tarp; the water tends to splash and drip—let's face it, this is a messy game!

Stand at the head of the lines with a quarter in your hand. Explain that you are going to flip the quarter so that only the first person in each line can see the results. The two who can see how the quarter lands can't yell out the result or even look back at their teams. If the quarter lands on tails, the leaders do nothing, but you should pause a moment after each flip to see if they will send a false message. If the quarter lands on heads, each leader will squeeze the hand of the player directly behind them. That player then squeezes the hand of the player behind them, and so on. If the last person in line has their hand squeezed, that will signal them to grab the soap out of the bucket. The first player to successfully retrieve the soap gets to advance to the front of the line.

Seems pretty simple, doesn't it? Well, it is—until you consider what happens when the message is wrongly communicated to the person in back, and they grab the soap only to find out that the quarter was actually tails. At that point the person in front must go to the back of the line.

The first team to get their entire team forward in line (i.e., the first leader is back in front of the line) wins. When the game is still going well, but has gone on for a while, transition to your next activity.

> **Important Game Principle:** Always stop a game while the going's good. In other words, stop it while kids want more, not when they've already tuned out. It's always good to leave them with the thought, *Hey, that was fun. I only wish we had more time. I can't wait till next week!*

FOOT TO EAR

This is similar to musical chairs, but much, much better—and all you need is music!

This game works best with an even number of guys and girls. (You can make other divisions work, but we're just going to use the guy/girl scenario for explanation purposes.) Have the girls stand in a circle; then have the guys stand outside of the circle of girls, each guy in back of one girl who will be his partner for the game. Have the inner circle (girls) walk clockwise when the music begins and the outer circle (guys) walk counterclockwise. When the music stops, yell out two body parts (e.g., "foot to ear"). The first body part belongs to the girls (ladies first) and the second to the guys. Huh? When the music stops and the leader yells the body parts, the partners need to run straight to each other and put those designated body parts together (e.g., the girl would run to the guy and put her foot on his ear). Great game—just think before you yell body parts (I'm sure you understand what I mean).

When you get down to the last two couples, it's nice to see how dedicated they are. You can yell out something like "lip to lip!"

THE BIG SQUEEZE

This game saved me quite a few times because I was always looking for games that would work for over 100 students. It's a good one for a big group (at least 20, but up to hundreds).

Quickly divide into two or more teams and announce that each team will be racing to squeeze into the shape of the item mentioned. For example: If the leader yells out the word "football," the teams must squeeze into the shape of a football as it would be seen from above. Keep score, first team to 10 wins. Here's some great squeeze shapes to call out:

- The state of California
- A dog
- A pair of sunglasses
- Jonathan (or whoever the leader is!)

- A baseball bat
- A shark
- A map of the U.S.A.

BIG BALLOON BOP

I normally wouldn't get so hyped up about a balloon game, but it leads into the next one so nicely. Go to your local art supply or party store and buy the biggest balloons they carry (16-inch ones are cool but 3-foot ones are better).

Here's what you'll need:

❏ Ten to 15 huge balloons
❏ Five pieces of paper, numbered 1 to 5 and stuffed into five of the balloons

Form two teams. As numerous staff members throw the balloons into the game, each team will try to hit the balloons over to the opposing team's side. After about five minutes, yell "Stop!" At this point tell students to pop the balloons. Have small pieces of paper with numbers on them in five of the balloons. Bring the students with the numbers up front to use for the next game!

LET'S MAKE A DEAL

I know this is an up-front game and might belong in chapter 2, but it flows so well from the last game. And I don't want to interrupt any *flowage*!

Here's what you'll need:

❏ A pocket filled with money (seriously!)
❏ An assistant or two who rehearsed with you
❏ Five boxes (all of the same size), each labeled with one of the following: "Box 1," "Box 2," "Box 3," "Box 4" and "Box 5"
❏ Five prizes

Draw five names from the audience or use the Big Balloon Bop to choose players. Have an assistant walk onstage with a big box labeled "Box 1." I told Contestant Number One that he could have the box or $10. He wanted the box. I dug in my pocket and offered him another $10, a total of $20. This went on until he finally took $40 cash. When we revealed what was in Box 1, everyone found out it only contained a $5 jar of licorice.

Contestant Number Two learned that previously the money was the better option. However, he chose Box 2 when it was offered. I offered him $40 and then $60. Some in the crowd were yelling, "Take the money!" Others yelled, "The box! The box!" He still demanded the box. Finally I offered him $80 cash, and he took it. We opened Box 2 to find a TV/VCR combo worth almost $200. The crowd went crazy!

Contestant Number Three was convinced that the box was a pretty good choice (wouldn't you be?)! After offering him $40 cash, I gave in and told him he could have the box. We opened it to reveal his prize: a TROUT! Yes, a cold dead fish! The crowd went crazy! You should have seen the poor kid's face.

Box 4 was a singing stuffed reindeer and Box 5 was a certificate to our next event. Fun stuff. I've never done it without first rehearsing the order with my assistant. The key is smooth transitions and knowing what's in each of the boxes!

ESTROGEN HOOP

This is a great time filler involving everyone, and it's simple.

Here's what you'll need:

- ❑ A basketball
- ❑ A basketball court (or level playing surface)

Have everyone (up to about 50 people) on the basketball court at once. Play normal basketball but with the following rules added:

- Only the girls can shoot or score.
- There's no limit to how many people can be on the court.

GUESS WHO

This game works for up to about 20 people.

Here's what you'll need:

- ❑ Paper, cut into small pieces
- ❑ Pens or pencils
- ❑ An easel with a newsprint pad of paper and a white board, chalkboard or a piece of poster board for displaying the list

Have everyone write a name (other than their own) on a piece of paper. Warn them that others will be trying to guess which name they wrote, so they should be discreet when writing the name. After the players have written the names, they fold their papers and pass them to the leader, who then mixes up the order of the slips and writes all the names on the easel (or whatever you use), making sure everyone can see the list.

The leader picks a student from the group (e.g., Frank)—not a name on the board—to start. Frank chooses another student and guesses what their name might be, saying something like "Bob, I think you wrote Cinderella." If Frank is correct, Bob is now on Frank's team, and Frank gets to guess again. If Frank is wrong, then it's Bob's turn to guess. Bob might ask Julie, "Julie, are you Abraham Lincoln?" If Julie wrote Abraham Lincoln, she joins Bob's team, and Bob guesses someone else. If not, it's now Julie's turn.

Once teams form, they work together to get other people onto their team. Play continues until all but one player has been guessed, and that person ends up being the player with everyone on his team.

SILENT ANIMAL CIRCLE

This game is really fun. It sounds goofy, but I've had kids from gangs playing this game and having a blast. It's perfect for smaller groups, leadership retreats, etc. It gets difficult with more than 20 people; it's better for groups of 8 to 15.

For this one, have everyone gather in a circle and assign each player an animal and a hand motion that represents it. Here are a few examples:

- **Elephant:** Hang one arm down with your other arm wrapped around it, holding your nose—there's your trunk!

- **Mosquito:** Use your left hand to make a peace sign with the inside of your hand facing you. With your right hand, poke your index finger pointing forward and place it in the middle of the peace sign in your left hand. Now bring your hands up to your face—you now have a mosquito nose!
- **Cow:** Put your hand on your stomach with your fingers sticking out like an udder—need I say more?
- **Deer:** Point each hand's index finger upward and place your hands on top of your head—now you've got deer antlers.
- **Moose:** Open your hands with your fingers spread wide and place your hands on your head with thumbs touching the top of your head. (Hey, Rocky!)

Let's say that 12 people are playing this game and everyone is in a circle. Whoever is in the 12 o'clock position of the circle is the elephant, and the elephant is the leader. In the 11 o'clock position is the mosquito; after that you can do the animals in whatever order you like. Here's the key: the *animals* don't change position; as people move, they assume the role of the animal in that particular spot. The object is to get to be the elephant. As people mess up in this game, they have to move back to the 1 o'clock position and work their way up again as others mess up.

The elephant starts the game by doing his own signal, then another animal's signal, such as the cow. The cow must then do her own signal and another animal's signal immediately. A certain rhythm or speed is set by the elephant (by how fast he does the signals). Everyone must keep that rhythm—no hesitations. If an individual pauses, forgets to do their signal or messes up the signal in any way, then they must go back to the 1 o'clock position.

Huh?! OK, let's say that the cow is always in the 10 o'clock position. If the person that was the cow messes up, then he or she goes to the 1 o'clock position to be a different animal, for example a snake. The person who was in the 9 o'clock position is now the cow and so on down the line. Whenever someone messes up, it is only the people below them who are affected and have to move up to a new animal. If the elephant messes up, everyone moves because he is the highest position.

REAL IDENTITY

This is a great getting-to-know-ya memory game. I always play it at the beginning of the year when I have a bunch of new students. This game helps me learn their names.

Have everyone sit in a circle and take turns saying their names and something about themselves (e.g., "Hi, I'm John and I play football"). The next person needs to repeat the previous person's name and item of interest before saying their own (e.g., "He's John, he plays football, and I'm Mary—I collect stuffed animals"). As this game moves on, people need to remember more and more information. With bigger groups you can have them only repeat the names in order to save time.

NEWSPAPER NAME SMACK

Sad but true: when in doubt, resort to beating each other with objects. Students love this! This game is usually better for groups of less than 30.

Here's what you'll need:

❑ Two rolled-up newspapers (one for backup when the first gets shredded) or a pillow.

Put everyone in a circle. I have everyone around the circle say their names; then I grab a rolled-up newspaper and ask, "Who would like to take a whack at a friend?" After choosing someone (from a lot of raised hands, as I'm sure you've already guessed), I explain the goal at hand (and notice I still haven't called this a game).

Here's how it goes: Have each person give their name again, making sure everyone says their name clearly so that all others can hear it. Start the game by calling the name of someone in the room and have them stand in the middle of the circle with the rolled-up newspaper. Call out another name, and the person in the middle proceeds to find that person and tries to whack 'em with the rolled-up newspaper (or pillow) before that person can say both their name, and someone else's name in the room. If they get whacked before they can say their name and someone else's name, they are now It. The person who is in the middle takes the place in the circle of the person they whacked. This helps people learn each others' names and mixes everyone around. Great fun, and students love it!

ANKLE-BALLOON POP

Here's what you'll need:

❑ Enough balloons for everyone
❑ Enough *precut* (remember Deadly Sin Number Two on page 13) 18-inch pieces of string or yarn for everyone

Give everyone a balloon and a piece of string or yarn. Have everyone blow up their balloons and tie them to their ankles. When everyone's ready, announce that they must try to stomp out other people's balloons while keeping their own safe. The last person with an intact balloon wins.

STEAL THE BACON HOCKEY-STYLE

This one's great! Again, remember *not* to say, "Now we're going to play a game!" (remember Deadly Sin Number One?). Just announce that you need everyone to stand in twos and start numbering them off (do this quickly—after all, you don't want to commit Deadly Sin Number Five!).

Here's what you'll need:

❑ Ten or so hockey sticks
❑ A ball (any soft ball, such as a tennis ball, will work)

This is a form of the traditional Steal the Bacon. After the group has been split into two teams (or four, if you're brave, placing the teams in a square), line each team along the sidelines of the play area and number them off. Teams must be even, so each person has a corresponding opponent with the same number across the play area. Place approximately 10 hockey sticks and a small ball in the middle of the play area. Specify one wall as the direction one team will go and the opposite wall for the other.

Yell out a number (11, for example). Both number 11s run out, pick up a hockey stick and try to hit the ball toward their specified wall (or goal). The first one to hit the goal wins the match.

This game gets more interesting when you yell out multiple numbers (e.g., 3, 7, 13 and 15). You end up with a little hockey match.

PULL APART

This is the heinous game in which all the guys link up by getting in a big pile, hugging and grabbing each other—whatever is necessary—in order to stay connected. When you say "Go," the girls try to pull them apart. Once a guy is pulled away from the pile (i.e., when he isn't touching anyone in the pile anymore), he's out and must go sit down. The last two guys linked together are the winners.

I don't suggest reversing the gender roles in this game. Guys don't need to be grabbing girls. They'll think about it for weeks!

TAPE HEAD

This is one of the best games you can play with a crowd.

Here's what you'll need:

- ❑ A hat for each runner
- ❑ Lots of tape to make sticky hats (wrap tape around the hats, sticky side up)

The up-front person (the emcee) divides the group into teams (with large groups you can group by section). Each team designates a runner who stands in front of their section, wearing a sticky hat. The emcee then yells out a demand for a common item that people might have with them. The team finds that item and sticks it on their runner's head. The first runner who makes it up to the emcee with the item stuck to their head wins that round. Make sure there's a lot of tape on the hats. The following are some good items to call for:

- A shoelace
- A student body card
- A piece of chewed gum
- Three belts hooked together
- Three necklaces tied together
- A picture of a baby
- A driver's license
- A $20 bill
- A *self-plucked* red hair
- A handwritten note

Teams must leave the items stuck on the hat until the end of the game. Great fun! Take pictures!

WHO'S ON MY BACK?

This is a great game that forces everyone to go around and meet other people.

Here's what you'll need:

- ❏ Small pieces of paper for everyone
- ❏ Pens or pencils for everyone
- ❏ Transparent or masking tape

Have everyone secretly write down the name of a famous person on a small piece of paper. It has to be someone that everyone in the room would know (e.g., Jesus, George Washington, Britney Spears, Brad Pitt, etc.). After they've written the person's name (making sure no one sees it), they will tape it on the back of the person to their left. Everyone must now go around and ask people yes-or-no questions about whose name is on their back. They can only ask each person one question. The person who guesses the name on their back in the least number of tries wins.

> **Note:** You can find other games that relate to a specific topic in the next chapter.

Do You Have Any Ready-Made Youth Group Agendas?

COMPLETE, READY-TO-USE MIDWEEK OUTLINES

It's Tuesday night, and your program starts in just under an hour. You meant to plan yesterday, but you didn't expect all these phone calls. Today you got slammed at work. One thing led to another, and here you are with *nothing* planned!

You're away from your computer. CRUD! You forgot to go to that website that bails you out if you forgot to plan—no ready-made agendas this week! You're short on time, you're offline, and you really should spend the remainder of your time praying! What do you do? Well, here's a bunch of good program agendas you can use.

AGENDA LAYOUT

The majority of the following agendas are outlined the same way. They provide flexibility to adjust to your planned schedule and crowd size. You'll want to customize these agendas with appropriate games and discussion formats. The games for a group of 10 in a home are going to be different than games for 200 in a gym, so adjust accordingly.

Most of the agendas were written for a weekly program with the purpose of outreach. The discussions can work for a growth/discipleship crowd as well, but may need to be altered.

The following are descriptions of the headings you'll find in these agendas:

TOPIC

All the agendas start with the topic. The topic is simply the subject of discussion for that night. The topic might be friendship, family, sex or choices—you name it; it's the subject of discussion for the program.

MAIN POINT

The main point is the purpose of the meeting. Each member of my staff gets a copy of the agenda so that they keep the focus throughout the meeting.

SUPPLIES

I like to be able to glance at the top of my program agenda and know exactly what I need for that evening. One thing I am never without is what I call the Basic Info Card. These are little cards that I use to collect information on new and visiting students—such as name, address, phone, pager and/or cell numbers, e-mail address, school, grade and birthday. It can also include fun stuff like favorite movie, favorite music and favorite thing to do for fun. (**Note:** You'll find a reproducible version of the Basic Info Card on page 205. Simply copy onto cardstock and cut the cards to size; then keep 'em handy!)

Hint: Notice that I mentioned getting an e-mail address. This does two things: first, it tells you a little about the student. Students usually will choose an e-mail identity that represents who they are now or what they want to be. You may discover that the nice, new, innocent-looking girl in your group has an e-mail address of g-stringdiva@???.com; or you might have a student leader who has the address player@???.com (and he's not talking about playing soccer!). A lot of these addresses are about the image students want to project and can be little windows into who they are. I've had middle-class, preppy kids with e-mail addresses like gangster@???.com.

The second reason I like to ask for e-mail addresses is simply that it's fun to contact students via e-mail. You can set up e-mail lists to update students concerning activities and events. Also, some students will open up to you via e-mail more than they will in person. A growing number of young people have no interpersonal skills and are developing most of their social skills in chat rooms on the Web.

Asking students about their favorite movie, music and thing to do for fun informs you about the kinds of things students are putting into their heads. This kind of information is excellent for staff members to have while trying to build relationships with students.

BASIC INFO CARD

Your Name _____   Today's Date _____

Address _____

Phone _____   E-mail _____

School _____   Grade _____

Birth Date _____

Parent/Guardian's Name _____

STUDENTS ARRIVE

Students love to just hang out with each other. Provide a time to do that and keep it flexible, depending on the facility you have. Basketball courts and foosball tables might allow more time for this than just hanging out in someone's living room. Instruct staff members to make students feel welcome during this time. Introduce yourself to students you haven't yet met and give new students a Basic Info Card to fill out.

BRING IT TOGETHER

Finally, at a given time you should bring it together (usually about 15 minutes after start time). Gather everyone together and start the program. I usually start with a "Hey, glad to see you all here. Welcome to (name of youth group)!"

INTRODUCE NEW PEOPLE

Every week I have the new students announce their names and the schools they attend. Train student leaders to use this as a time to cheer and make new people feel welcome, even if they attend a rival school. It's amazing how a core group of students can determine the atmosphere that a youth group has. I've been to youth groups where it was almost scary for students to wear a rival school's letterman jacket. Create an atmosphere where students in rival jackets are sitting next to each other, laughing and having a good time.

Give every new person a Blow-Pop, Skittles, a Snickers bar or something similar. The goal is to let visitors know that you are genuinely glad they've come. And, to put it simply, kids like candy!

YOUTH CHALLENGE

Most programs should start with up-front games right off the bat. This focuses attention on the stage immediately and gets the evening going with something fun. Usually I have two students come up and do a challenge against each other, such as Soda Slam, Surgical Glove Blowup, Joust or just a simple burping contest (just in case you skipped it, check out chapter 2 for more on up-front games). Be creative!

ANNOUNCEMENTS

After you've had some fun with an up-front game, make announcements. Every youth group has announcements of upcoming activities, events and trips. This can also be a good time to recognize birthdays.

GAME

Rarely will I run a program without some kind of game. Games are great for so many reasons. They open kids up and allow them to laugh. They give students an opportunity to interact and laugh with each other. Games allow staff members to team up with students and bond with them. Games break down walls (sometimes literally!).

I don't always specify games on these agendas. Sometimes I'll just tell you to choose a game from the games listed in this book, online at thesourcefym.com or from your own game list. Occasionally, though, I'll list a specific game that relates to a particular discussion.

DISCUSSION STARTER

A discussion starter is usually a video clip, a drama, a story or some sort of survey or worksheet for students to fill out. This usually segues to the topic by provoking discussion on the subject.

SMALL-GROUP QUESTIONS

I like to use small groups to discuss the topic for the evening. The majority of these program agendas provide small-group questions if you want to use them. Many times these questions can also be discussed with the whole group as well.

Read chapter 7 for more information on the benefits of using small groups as part of or in addition to your weekly meetings.

WRAP-UP

The wrap-up is the final talk summarizing the main point. I usually like to do this with the whole group, as opposed to each small group doing their own.

CLOSING PRAYER

It seems obvious, but always close your meetings in prayer. It's great to have student-led prayer if students are willing, but don't force anyone to do it. Incorporate the meeting topic into the prayer, challenging students to apply it to their lives, and thank God for the chance to come together.

> **Note:** The reproducible pages listed in the following agendas can be found in appendix *B* at the back of the book.

Program Agenda One

GOD IS THE ULTIMATE, LOVING FATHER

TOPIC

Family

MAIN POINT

Sometimes our families aren't all we wish they were, but our heavenly Father is always there for us, regardless of our own shortcomings.

KEY VERSE

"But God demonstrates his own love for us in this: While we were still sinners, Christ died for us." Romans 5:8

SUPPLIES

❑ Paper
❑ Pens or pencils
❑ Props for games

STUDENTS ARRIVE

• Make everyone feel welcome.
• Learn names and interests of newcomers.
• Give each newcomer a Basic Info Card (see p. 205).

BRING IT TOGETHER

About 15 minutes after start time, welcome students and start the program.

INTRODUCE NEW PEOPLE

Distribute candy to the newcomers and welcome them to the group.

YOUTH CHALLENGE

Choose an up-front game. Invite two students to volunteer and challenge one another. (Some examples are: Soda Slam, Surgical Glove Blowup and Joust.) Be creative!

ANNOUNCEMENTS

Announce upcoming activities and events and honor birthdays.

GAME

Choose a game from the game list.

DISCUSSION STARTER

Drama

Explain that you need some volunteers to role-play given situations that occur in a common American household. Describe the first situation; then ask who would like to play the characters for that scenario. Be sure to choose students who would be good at thinking on the spot and assuming the role of a character. Let the volunteers act out their scenes; then choose volunteers for the next situation and so on.

- **Situation One:** Last night the son or daughter came home an hour late. It's breakfast and the subject is being discussed.
- **Situation Two:** The family is sitting down discussing the oldest brother's or sister's future. The parents see college—the student sees a job and living with friends.
- **Situation Three:** The subject of dating has come up at the dinner table. The son or daughter has been dating the same person for a long time now, and the parents want to make sure that he or she is being careful (i.e., the sex issue or the dating-one-person-too-much issue).

SMALL-GROUP QUESTIONS

Form small groups, and give everyone a small piece of paper and a pencil or pen. Have them fold the paper in half and then again, and then a third time so that they end up with six small squares. This is a drawing exercise. Assure kids that this is not meant to test their artistic ability; it's just a way to creatively express feelings. They may just draw a stick figure or a symbol; it's up to them. Give the following directions:

1. **In box 1, draw a letter, a symbol or a picture of the first thing that comes to your mind when you think of your dad.** (Give them ideas of what they could draw, e.g., "If you play sports with your dad, you can draw a basketball; if your dad isn't around much, you can draw an empty house; if your dad is always giving you things, you can draw a gift.")

2. **In box 2, draw a letter, a symbol or a picture of the first thing that comes to mind when you think of your mom.**

3. **In box 3, draw a horizontal line. On the left side of the line write "closer" and on the right side of the line write "away." Now place yourself as a dot on the line indicating which direction you are moving in your relationship with one or both of your parents—you choose. Are you drawing closer to them or moving farther away?**

4. **In box 4, draw a letter, a symbol or a picture of something you would do the same way that your parents do if you were in their shoes.**

5. **In box 5, draw a letter, a symbol or a picture of something that you would do differently from your parents if you were in their shoes.**

6. **In box 6, draw a picture of something that represents the perfect relationship with a parent.**

Now students will share within their small groups. Each person should share six separate times, once for each box. Encourage them to briefly share their drawings and what they mean.

WRAP-UP

Alec's Mess

Share the following case study:

> Alec's dad was thirsty and asked if four-year-old Alec would get him a drink. Alec tried his best, but in the process he knocked stuff out of the fridge, spilled the milk, broke a glass, and finally tripped and spilled his dad's drink all over the living room floor. Alec's dad didn't get mad. In fact, he helped Alec clean up the mess because he saw that Alec was trying hard to please his dad.

Expand on this story in your own words and storytelling style; then summarize by sharing: **I mess up a lot in life. But I always know that God is still going to be there for me. Although it makes Him sad when I mess things up for myself, He still loves me. Some of you don't get the kind of love that Alec's father showed him in the story. The good news is that this is the kind of love God can give to us.**

CLOSING PRAYER

Close in prayer, thanking God for His love and praying for His protection and guidance in the coming week.

Program Agenda Two

BROKEN HOMES, MENDED HEARTS

TOPIC
Family strife

MAIN POINT
Our families may go through rough times, but our loving heavenly Father will always be there to love and comfort us.

KEY VERSES
"So he got up and went to his father.

"But while he was still a long way off, his father saw him and was filled with compassion for him; he ran to his son, threw his arms around him and kissed him.

"The son said to him, 'Father, I have sinned against heaven and against you. I am no longer worthy to be called your son.'

"But the father said to his servants, 'Quick! Bring the best robe and put it on him. Put a ring on his finger and sandals on his feet.'" Luke 15:20-22

SUPPLIES
❑ The video *Stepmom* (Columbia Pictures, 1998)
❑ A TV and a VCR
❑ Six pieces of paper labeled with one of the following: "Dad," "Mom," "Older Bro," "Middle Child," "Little Sis" and "Stepdad"
❑ React Cards (blank 3x5-inch index cards)
❑ Approximately 15 to 20 blank pieces of paper
❑ A felt-tip pen
❑ Pens or pencils
❑ Lots of newspaper
❑ Several rolls of tape
❑ Props for games

STUDENTS ARRIVE

- Make everyone feel welcome.
- Learn names and interests of newcomers.
- Give each newcomer a Basic Info Card (see p. 205).

BRING IT TOGETHER

About 15 minutes after start time, welcome students and start the program.

INTRODUCE NEW PEOPLE

Distribute candy to the newcomers and welcome them to the group.

YOUTH CHALLENGE

Choose an up-front game. Invite two students to volunteer and challenge one another. (Some examples are: Soda Slam, Surgical Glove Blowup and Joust.) Be creative!

ANNOUNCEMENTS

Announce upcoming activities and events and honor birthdays.

GAME

Choose a game from the game list and/or use the following game:

The Big Bad Wolf

Divide students into groups of three. Give each group a small stack of newspapers and some tape, and instruct them to build a newspaper shelter. The shelter must be big enough to allow all three team members inside. The wolf or wolves (staff) then attempt to blow the shelter down. Afterward, have a giant paper fight.

Option: Use the game to begin a brief talk about how many American homes are falling apart—not structurally, but as a family unit.

DISCUSSION STARTER

Select five students to represent family members in a typical American family. No acting is required here; they simply have to hold up signs when given the cue. Assign each of the volunteers one of the roles, and stick a sign on them indicating who they're portraying.

Give a helper the felt-tip pen, tape and 15 to 20 pieces of paper so that you're ready to write down the responsibilities of each family member. Ask the group: **So what does a Dad do?** Answers may range from "Nothing!" to "Beats his kids!" to "Goes to work!" Try to filter the joke answers and encourage the truthful ones. Find something reasonable such as: **So would everybody agree that the average family has Dad as the primary wage earner?** Write "$" on a piece of paper and stick it on Dad (with tape) if the audience agrees. Follow that up with **Cool. Is the dad also the main one who handles discipline?** If so, write "discipline" on a piece of paper and stick it on Dad. Repeat the steps for each family member until each has several pieces of paper stuck on them.

Here's an idea of what different family members might have stuck to them:

- Dad: $, discipline, money, yard care, wash car, fix stuff
- Mom: $, grocery shopping, nurture, clean house, laundry
- Older Bro: Chores, beating up siblings
- Middle Child: Baby-sitting, fun
- Little Sis: No responsibilities

Continue: **Now if this is the typical home in America, let's say that Dad leaves.** Tear up Dad's sign, pull off all of Dad's responsibilities signs, and have the volunteer sit down. **Now we have to transfer Dad's responsibilities to the rest of the family.** Holding up the $ piece of paper ask: **Who is going to replace the income?** Be prepared for answers such as "A boyfriend!" or "Alimony!" Reel 'em back in: **Could some of this financial responsibility fall on Mom? Maybe she's already working, either part time or full time. She's going to have to increase her working hours to earn more money, right? Let's give some of that responsibility to Older Brother too.** Tear the $ paper in half; then tape half on Mom and half on Older Brother. Divide the rest of the responsibilities, and adjust everyone else's responsibilities so that they balance. Those little pieces of paper being switched from person to person and the adding of more responsibilities on each family member demonstrate the drastic effects of divorce in a very visual way.

Now what if a stepdad shows up? Bring up a new guy from the audience and put the "Stepdad" sign on him. **What responsibilities does he take? Does he marry the mom or does he marry the whole family?** This question affects whether the rest of the family relies on him to take responsibilities. If there is no trust, then there probably is no transfer except from Mom. Continue discussion and switching as desired.

WRAP-UP

Use the video clip from *Stepmom* as outlined in the next chapter (p. 112). Then tell a rehearsed modern-day story of the prodigal son. Conclude by explaining that what you just told was a modern retelling of a story Jesus told in the Bible: **Jesus told this story so we could get a glimpse of what God is like. God is a loving Father who forgives all the bad things we have done and who cares for us deeply. He's waiting for each of us with His arms wide open, waiting to say, "Welcome home, My son. Welcome home, My daughter."**

> **Note:** Don't whip up this story five minutes before you do it; make sure you rehearse it (did ya read chapter 1?!). The responses you ask for are going to be based largely on this story. You'll want a clear picture of a loving Father who's willing to forgive the past and welcome us home.

Pass out the React Cards—I know, these are just blank index cards, but I call them React Cards because they allow students to write down their reaction to the discussion. Invite students to write their names and phone numbers on the card. Continue: **Write the number 1 on the card and then stop and listen.** Pause to let them write the number. **How does it make you feel that you have a loving, forgiving heavenly Father like the one we just talked about? Write your thoughts next to the number 1.** Conclude with: **If you are interested in talking to someone about having a relationship with God, write down the number 2 and next to it, write the word "yes."** Now fold your card in half, hold it in the air and we'll pick it up. Please let us know if you have any questions about tonight's subject; we'll be happy to answer them.

CLOSING PRAYER

Take this time to thank God for being the loving Father He is, and pray for those youth who said yes to God tonight. Praise God for all He is doing in your group, in your church and in the world.

> **Note:** Be sure to contact—or have another adult staff member contact—any of the students who noted on their React Cards that they want to talk to someone about having a relationship with God. Or invite those students to come talk to you or another staff member right after dismissal from this meeting.

Program Agenda Three

TRUE FRIENDSHIP

TOPIC

Friends

MAIN POINT

True friendships are important, and God wants to be our best friend.

KEY VERSES

"My command is this: Love each other as I have loved you. Greater love has no one than this, that he lay down his life for his friends." John 15:12-13

SUPPLIES

❑ 32 blank sheets of paper and a felt-tip pen

❑ Props for games

❑ A prize for the game (optional)

STUDENTS ARRIVE

• Make everyone feel welcome.

• Learn names and interests of newcomers.

• Give each newcomer a Basic Info Card (see p. 205).

BRING IT TOGETHER

About 15 minutes after start time, welcome students and start the program.

INTRODUCE NEW PEOPLE

Distribute candy to the newcomers and welcome them to the group.

YOUTH CHALLENGE

Choose an up-front game. Invite two students to volunteer and challenge one another. (Some examples are: Soda Slam, Surgical Glove Blowup and Joust.) Be creative!

ANNOUNCEMENTS

Announce upcoming activities and events and honor birthdays.

GAME

The Friendship Game

This game is played like the old game show *The Newlywed Game*. Pick four pairs of students as contestants. The best mix is two guys, two girls, a guy and a girl who are friends and a guy and a girl who are dating. This way you have four different kinds of friendships represented. If you don't have this mix, do your best with what you have. Designate one person from each pair as *A* and the other as *B*. Have a staff person take the *A*s out of the room so they cannot hear. Ask the remaining contestants the Set *A* Questions, and have a staff person write down each answer on a full sheet of paper and order in such a way as to allow the person to pick up each answer in succession from a facedown position. Bring back the *A*s and ask them the same questions, showing their partner's answers and keeping track of each team's points. When you finish (time permitting), take the *B*s out of the room and do the same thing, using the Set *B* questions.

> **Note:** Make sure you word the questions correctly (e.g., **What did your friend say *you* would say to the following question?**).

Scoring is any way you wish; for instance, you might want to assign fewer points to the first few questions and more points to the last ones. Whoever has the most points at the end wins. You can award a fun prize if you wish.

Set *A* Questions

1. What will your friend say is their favorite thing to do for fun?
2. What will your friend say is the most embarrassing thing that happened to you both together?
3. Which of the following will your friend say best describes your friendship?
   a. A sailboat
   b. A roller coaster
   c. The weather
4. Which of the following will your friend say is most important in a relationship?
   a. Talking with each other
   b. Doing things together
   c. Never arguing

Set *B* Questions

1. What will your friend say is your best stupid-human trick?
2. Which of the following will your friend say they value most about you?
   a. You're dependable
   b. You're honest
   c. You listen
3. Which of the following ways will your friend say they handle conflict?
   a. Like a gangster
   b. Like a politician
   c. Like a comedian
4. Which of the following will your friend say is most destructive of friendships?
   a. Dishonesty
   b. Insecurity
   c. Gossip

Small-Group Questions

1. Think of one of your friends for a moment. What qualities do you like about that friend?
2. What are some of the benefits of friendship?
3. What are some good reasons that people might seek friendship? What are some bad reasons?
4. Think of several of your friends right now. What, if anything, would cause them to stop being your friends?
5. What are you willing to sacrifice to build a friendship?
6. How can someone you don't know show you friendship qualities? (For example, a stranger helps you when you get hurt; someone on the staff makes you feel welcome when you visit the group for the first time; you receive a scholarship from a person or group you don't even know.)
7. Can you see God as your friend? Why or why not?
8. How could you keep up a friendship with God?

Wrap-Up

You may want to start with a story of someone who sacrificed something for a friend—a personal story is great. Explain: **The Bible says something really cool about friendship in John 15:12-13: "Love each other as I have loved you. Greater love has no one than this, that he lay down his life for his friends." Jesus shows us what true friendship is; it is measured by the degree of sacrifice. When we enter into a relationship with God through Jesus, we become His friend. He has already proven the depth of His commitment of friendship with us by paying the price for our rebellion against Him. He gave everything He had to give when He sacrificed His life for us.**

Through a relationship with God we see the best example ever of what a true friend is and how we too can sacrifice our lives daily in little ways, by dying to self, not just by being willing to die for someone. Our friendship with God shows when we love others the way God loves us.

CLOSING PRAYER

Thank God for loving each one present and giving His Son so that all might have eternal life with Him. Pray that He will give each of you the opportunity to share His love with someone this week.

Program Agenda Four

OUR FUTURE IN QUESTION

TOPIC

The future

MAIN POINT

Each of us must take required steps to reach the future God intends for us.

KEY VERSE

" 'For I know the plans I have for you,' declares the LORD, 'plans to prosper you and not to harm you, plans to give you hope and a future.' "
Jeremiah 29:11

SUPPLIES

❑ The Small-Group Questions
❑ Copies of "Goal Sheet—Where I Want to Be in the Future" (p. 206)
❑ Pens or pencils
❑ Props for games

STUDENTS ARRIVE

• Make everyone feel welcome.
• Learn names and interests of newcomers.
• Give each newcomer a Basic Info Card (see p. 205).

BRING IT TOGETHER

About 15 minutes after start time, welcome students and start the program.

INTRODUCE NEW PEOPLE

Distribute candy to the newcomers and welcome them to the group.

YOUTH CHALLENGE

Choose an up-front game. Invite two students to volunteer and challenge one another. (Some examples are: Soda Slam, Surgical Glove Blowup and Joust.) Be creative!

ANNOUNCEMENTS

Announce upcoming activities and events and honor birthdays.

GAME

Choose a game from the games list.

DISCUSSION STARTER

Distribute copies of "Goal Sheet—Where I Want to Be in the Future" and pens or pencils. Give students time to complete their questionnaires.

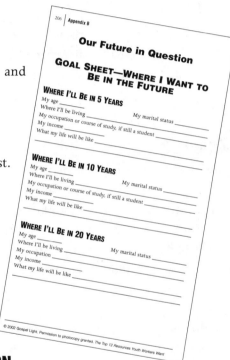

SMALL-GROUP DISCUSSION

Have students share what they wrote, using the following questions:

1. Where do you think you will be in 5 years, 10 years and 20 years?
2. What was the hardest item for you to predict?
3. Do some of these predictions make you think about the decisions that you will make today?

Discuss the following generic questions regarding the future:

1. Do you feel the future is getting better or worse? Why?
2. Do you think your future life will be better than that of your parents? Why?
3. What factors/ingredients influence your future the most?
4. Who has the greatest influence on your future?
5. How are you responsible for your future?
6 How do your decisions impact your future?
7. What is something you've done during this school year (good, bad, major, minor) that affects who you are today?
8. Can your decisions impact someone else's future? How?

Wrap-Up

Lead into the good news of the gospel: **Listening to everyone talk, I've heard that different people affect your future. I've also heard that you and the decisions you make are going to have a huge impact on your future. A long time ago God made a huge choice that has an incredible impact on your future.** Share the gospel as presented in appendix A beginning on page 196.

After you have gone through the presentation of the gospel, lead into the closing prayer by explaining: **God is calling each of us into relationship with Him. Some of you may hear His voice right now. I pray that you will open your hearts to how God is moving in your life. The decision you make today will impact your future for eternity.**

Closing Prayer

Thank God for loving us enough to send His Son to die for us. Pray that the message the Lord wants to bring today will draw His children home and that they will know the truth of the good news.

Program Agenda Five

OUR PAST FORGIVEN

TOPIC

Our past

MAIN POINT

God doesn't hold our past against us; He's forgiven our sin and cares about the direction we're headed.

KEY VERSES

"Repent, then, and turn to God, so that your sins may be wiped out, that times of refreshing may come from the Lord." Acts 3:19

SUPPLIES

❑ Props for games
❑ A bedsheet

STUDENTS ARRIVE

• Make everyone feel welcome.
• Learn names and interests of newcomers.
• Give each newcomer a Basic Info Card (see p. 205).

BRING IT TOGETHER

About 15 minutes after start time, welcome students and start the program.

INTRODUCE NEW PEOPLE

Distribute candy to the newcomers and welcome them to the group.

YOUTH CHALLENGE

Choose an up-front game. Invite two students to volunteer and challenge one another. (Some examples are: Soda Slam, Surgical Glove Blowup and Joust.) Be creative!

ANNOUNCEMENTS

Announce upcoming activities and events and honor birthdays.

GAME

Choose a game from the games list.

WHOLE-GROUP DISCUSSION

The Adulterous Woman (John 8:1-11)

> **On a Personal Note:** "I've used this thought provoker with groups of unchurched kids who don't know the Bible, and I've used it with adults with cemetery—oops! seminary—degrees." —JM

Read John 8:1-11 aloud. Ask for 6 to 10 volunteers to act out the different parts of this passage as you read. They won't have to act as much as they will be asked to consider what the person they're portraying might be thinking or doing at that moment. Assign the following roles: Jesus, a group of teachers of the law, a group of Pharisees and the adulterous woman (give her a bedsheet to wrap around her). The audience can be the crowd gathered around Jesus. Share the story as outlined and ask questions as the story unfolds. Begin by reading John 8:1-3:

> **But Jesus went to the Mount of Olives. At dawn he appeared again in the temple courts, where all the people gathered around him, and he sat down to teach them. The teachers of the law and the Pharisees brought in a woman caught in adultery. They made her stand before the group.**

Discuss:

1. **Why did these religious snobs bring this woman to Jesus?** (Because they were trying to trap Jesus [see v. 6].)

2. **Since they were trying to trap Jesus, how do you suppose they caught a woman committing adultery?** (The woman was probably set up.)

3. **If this was an act of adultery, where was the man?** (Since this was a setup, he was probably in on it.)

4. *Direct this question to the person portraying the woman* (wrapped in a bedsheet as though she is not clothed): **How do you feel standing there in front of everyone?** (Ashamed, scared.)

Read John 8:4-6:

> [They] said to Jesus, "Teacher, this woman was caught in the act of adultery. In the Law Moses commanded us to stone such women. Now what do you say?" They were using this question as a trap, in order to have a basis for accusing him.

Share that the teachers of the law and the Pharisees thought that they had come up with something Jesus could never get out of. Continue: **No matter which way He answered, they were sure they had Him cornered. If He answered, "Stone her," He was in trouble with Roman law, which forbade local governments from imposing the death penalty without permission (which is why they brought Jesus to Pilate later). If He answered, "Let her go," He would be going against the Mosaic law.** Read John 8:6:

> But Jesus bent down and started to write on the ground with his finger.

Discuss:

1. **Where has all the attention been since the woman was dragged in here? In other words, who has everybody been staring at?** (The attention was probably on the woman waiting to be stoned and on Jesus.)

---

2. Now that Jesus is writing on the ground, where is all the attention? *Directed to the crowd:* Now what are you looking at? (What Jesus is writing.)

3. The Bible never tells us what it is that Jesus wrote in the ground; why do you think it's important to this incident?

4. *Directed to the woman:* How do you feel now?

Read John 8:7-8:

> When they kept on questioning him, he straightened up and said to them, "If any one of you is without sin, let him be the first to throw a stone at her." Again he stooped down and wrote on the ground.

1. *Directed to the religious snobs:* What are you thinking now? (Uh-oh! Maybe He knows what we did; we can't stone her now.)

2. *Directed to the woman*: What are you thinking now?

3. *Directed to the crowd:* What are you thinking?

Read John 8:9:

> At this, those who heard began to go away one at a time, the older ones first, until only Jesus was left, with the woman still standing there.

Direct the following question to the woman: **What are you thinking now?** Allow for her response; then read John 8:10-11:

> Jesus straightened up and asked her, "Woman, where are they? Has no one condemned you?"
>
> "No one, sir," she said.
>
> "Then neither do I condemn you," Jesus declared. "Go now and leave your life of sin."

Explain that Jesus knew everything about the woman: **Basically He was saying, "I know where you've been and what you've done, but I** forgive you. Now I care about where you are going." Jesus is saying the same thing to us: "I know where you've been, and I forgive you. Now I care about where you are going." Thanks to the love, forgiveness and healing of Christ, how we walked in the door to this meeting doesn't matter anymore—although how we leave does.

CLOSING PRAYER

Thank God that He sent Jesus to die for our sin and that He loves us. Pray that all the mistakes and pain of our past will be wiped clean and that we will go out into the world knowing we are forgiven. Pray that that knowledge will call each of us to respond to God's grace and to walk away from our lives of sin.

Program Agenda Six

PIZZA-FEED OUTREACH

TOPIC

Pizza feed

MAIN POINT

Help students feel that this is a fun place to be—a great event for students to bring friends.

SUPPLIES

❏ Registration forms and pens or pencils
❏ A container for collecting registration forms
❏ Tables and chairs
❏ Pizza, lots of pizza!
❏ Several ice-filled coolers packed with soda
❏ Wheel o' Doom (see p. 29) and props for activities
❏ Game props
❏ A VCR and a projector unit with a giant screen
❏ A sound system for the video
❏ Giveaway items for the drawing: T-shirts, CDs, videos, toys, candy, scholarships to future events, certificates for lunch with staff, etc.

STUDENTS ARRIVE

• Make everyone feel welcome.
• Learn names and interests of newcomers.
• Give each newcomer a Basic Info Card (see p. 205).
• Serve pizza and sodas.

> **Note:** Avoid the self-serve situation where some students might take more than their fair share of the food and sodas, leaving little or nothing for those at the end of the line. Have adult staff members and/or parents available to monitor the amounts that students take. Events like this are great opportunities to involve parents and other church members.

BRING IT TOGETHER

About 15 minutes after start time, welcome students and start the program by explaining that you're going to give away some prizes to a few people who are sitting down and have good reflexes. All three of these games will get things moving!

Reflex Clap

Move your arms opposite each other, up and down in front of you, and explain that when your hands cross, the students are to clap their hands. Give a few practice tries and then fake them out by speeding up, slowing down, etc. Call for only upper classmen and then lower classmen to follow you. Be sure to give praise for their effort!

Ro-Sham-Bo Train

Have everyone grab a partner and play Rock, Paper, Scissors. The partner who loses goes behind the person who beat them, places their hands on the winner's shoulder and follows them around to find another pair to challenge. The losing pair gets behind the winning pair and so on until it's finally down to two huge trains. The winner of the last go-round is the one person in the room who never lost a round, and that person gets a prize.

The Wheel o' Doom

Begin a game of Wheel o' Doom (set up the wheel as described on page 29): **Who wants to be the first to give this thing a spin? OK, step right up and remember: Whatever the arrow lands on is what you have to do!** You can put a different spin on things by allowing contestants to choose someone to do certain activities with them. Great fun and a great way to make students really earn their prizes!

DISCUSSION

Use this time to address any new students: For those of you who are new to our youth group, we want you to know that we're here for you. We want this to be a place where you can come, be heard and express yourself. We'll always have a great time; sometimes we'll talk about things that are important to you, like friendship, family and the choices you make in life and how they affect you. And we're here to help you if you want it. Sometimes these talks will lead to discussions about God. Each of our staff members believes in God and has a relationship with Him. Don't worry, that doesn't mean anything funky—we won't pound on your heads with Bibles or make you sell flowers in airports or anything. We just believe a relationship with God is very important. If you have any questions about that, we'd love to try to answer them.

But most of all we're here for you and we're gonna have a blast this year, starting next week. We're gonna hand out flyers right now inviting you to bring your friends next week. Everyone who comes will get a root beer float!

INTRODUCE STAFF

Take a few minutes to introduce staff members to the group, giving them the opportunity to share a little bit about themselves. This helps the students to see the leaders as real people and will help the ministry to be a team of people who care about the kids.

WRAP-UP

Drawing

Have a drawing and give away some great prizes!

> **Optional Video Wrap-Up**
> Show an edited video of last year's events to give students a peek at the experiences they can enjoy as part of the group.

CLOSING PRAYER

Thank God for a great meeting and the opportunity to meet so many awesome new people. Pray that God will give everyone a safe and wonderful week.

CONCLUSION

Thanks for coming, and don't forget to be here next week at 7:00 P.M. (or whatever time you meet). **There'll be root beer floats for everyone!**

Program Agenda Seven

LOOKING OUT FOR NUMBER ONE

TOPIC
Priorities

MAIN POINT
We all have priorities in life; God wants to be at the top of your list of priorities.

KEY VERSES
"Therefore everyone who hears these words of mine and puts them into practice is like a wise man who built his house on the rock. The rain came down, the streams rose, and the winds blew and beat against that house; yet it did not fall, because it had its foundation on the rock. But everyone who hears these words of mine and does not put them into practice is like a foolish man who built his house on sand. The rain came down, the streams rose, and the winds blew and beat against that house, and it fell with a great crash." Matthew 7:24-27

SUPPLIES
❏ Props for games
❏ For every 5 to 6 students make one set of 18 Priority Cards—3x5-inch index cards labeled as follows:

- Study
- Athletic practice
- Go to youth group
- Call boyfriend/girlfriend
- Sleep a lot
- Read the Bible
- Attend classes at school

- Shop
- Watch TV
- Feed the dog/do chores
- Read a book
- Pray
- Go to church
- Go out with friends

- Talk with Mom
- Eat a lot
- Help a friend in trouble
- Help brother fix his bike

STUDENTS ARRIVE

- Make everyone feel welcome.
- Learn names and interests of newcomers.
- Give each newcomer a Basic Info Card (see p. 205).

BRING IT TOGETHER

About 15 minutes after start time, welcome students and start the program.

INTRODUCE NEW PEOPLE

Distribute candy to the newcomers and welcome them to the group.

YOUTH CHALLENGE

Choose an up-front game. Invite two students to volunteer and challenge one another. (Some examples are: Soda Slam, Surgical Glove Blowup and Joust.) Be creative!

ANNOUNCEMENTS

Announce upcoming activities and events and honor birthdays.

GAME

Choose a game from the game list.

SMALL GROUPS

Form small groups of five or six students, and give each group a set of Priority Cards. Have them lay the cards out; then put them in order of importance, with the most important first. Let the groups know that if there's not a unanimous agreement about the order of the list, the general consensus should be followed.

After each group has put its cards in order, ask what the reasoning behind certain decisions was. For instance, if "Talk with Mom" is way down on the list, create a scenario in which this might be a higher priority than its current location. If they put "Read the Bible" above "Watch TV," ask how many of them read their Bibles each day before they turn on the TV. (As a gauge of their spiritual commitment, note where groups put "Go to church," "Read the Bible" and "Pray.")

WRAP-UP

Explain that many people say that their priorities are in one order, and yet their actions reflect something else. The order of the Priority Cards probably made some in the group think about whether or not they liked the order of their own priorities. That's a good thing! Invite kids to talk with you sometime about their priorities: **If you want to talk to any of our staff, just let us know. You don't have to say that you want to talk, just a "Let's get a soda sometime" works! Hey, we'll even buy!**

CLOSING PRAYER

Thank God for bringing this group of great people together. Pray that He will help you keep your priorities in order and that the group members will always put Him at the top of their priority lists. Pray for a safe and wonderful week.

Program Agenda Eight

WHAT'S THE DEAL WITH SEX?

TOPIC
Sex

MAIN POINT
God created sex as a wonderful gift to be shared in marriage.

KEY VERSES
"It is God's will that you should be sanctified: that you should avoid sexual immorality; that each of you should learn to control his own body in a way that is holy and honorable, not in passionate lust like the heathen, who do not know God." 1 Thessalonians 4:3-5

SUPPLIES
- ❑ Copies of "Think About It" (pp. 207-208)
- ❑ Pens or pencils
- ❑ Props for games
- ❑ Gift certificate for fast food or ice cream with a leader

STUDENTS ARRIVE
- Make everyone feel welcome.
- Learn names and interests of newcomers.
- Give each newcomer a Basic Info Card (see p. 205).

BRING IT TOGETHER
About 15 minutes after start time, welcome students and start the program.

Introduce New People

Distribute candy to the newcomers and welcome them to the group.

Youth Challenge

Mommy Game

Here's what you'll need:

- ❏ Two fast-food or ice cream gift certificates
- ❏ Three large fabric squares (for diapers)
- ❏ Six diaper pins
- ❏ Three baby bottles (filled with milk, juice or water)
- ❏ Three jars of baby food
- ❏ Three spoons
- ❏ Three large sheets of paper
- ❏ Three large crayons

Hold up a gift certificate: **Who wants this certificate for a free lunch** (or whatever your certificate is for!)? **Great! I need three girls to grab a partner (male or female).** Once you have your three pairs, have the first partner play Mommy and the other partner play Baby. By the way, Baby can't talk! To win the prize, the mommies have to do everything on the following list. The first one to complete the tasks on the list wins a certificate for herself and her partner.

- Put a diaper on Baby while Baby lies on floor.
- Feed Baby a bottle.
- Burp Baby (Mommy leans Baby across Mommy's shoulder and pats Baby's back).
- Feed Baby a jar of baby food.
- Help Baby draw a picture of your house and family.
- Carry Baby to the crib (a designated spot in room).

Announcements

Announce upcoming activities and events and honor birthdays.

GAME

Choose a game from the games list.

DISCUSSION STARTER

Lead into the discussion by explaining: **The first game we played with moms and babies was funny, but it touched on an issue that is hitting teens across America: teen pregnancy. Girls are getting pregnant at increasingly younger ages. Many teens are convinced that condoms and other birth control methods are fail-safe, so they are having sex more often. The truth is that *no* birth-control method is fail-safe, and the only way to be completely safe is to abstain—which means *not having sex outside of marriage*. Teen pregnancies are up, diseases are up and the abortion rate has skyrocketed. We want to give you a chance to share your feelings or ask questions. And remember: There is no such thing as a stupid question here.**

Agree/Disagree

Designate one side of the room as the Agree side and the other side as the Disagree side. Read the following statements and have students respond by walking to the side of the room that indicates whether they agree or disagree. Don't be afraid to challenge the students by asking why they respond the way they do to some of the statements. You might have a staff member write down the score of Agrees and Disagrees for reference.

> A woman should
> - Always wear a dress.
> - Cry when Mufasa dies in *The Lion King*.
> - Get revenge when she is wronged.
> - Gossip about her experiences with men.
> - Wait for the man to open the door for her.
> - Have sex whenever it is offered to her and she wants it.
> - Have sex after a certain time period in a relationship.
> - Go through with having sex with a guy even if she changes her mind halfway through and doesn't want to go all the way.

- Feel obligated to have sex with a man if he buys her expensive things and tells her he loves her.
- Have sex with someone she loves.
- Wait to have sex until she is married.

A real man
- Likes sports.
- Doesn't cry.
- Gets revenge when he is wronged.
- Brags about his experiences with women.
- Opens doors for women.
- Has sex whenever it is offered to him and he wants it.
- Should expect sex after a certain time period in a relationship.
- Should go through with having sex with a girl even if the girl changes her mind halfway through and doesn't want to go all the way.
- Should always stop when a woman says no.
- Has sex with someone he loves.
- Waits to have sex until he is married.

DISCUSSION QUESTIONS

The questions on "Think About It" can be discussed with the whole group. Use your own discretion, considering the size and maturity of your group. If the group is large, you may want to divide by grade; if students are a less-mature group (typically sixth, seventh and/or eighth graders), it might be better to divide by grade *and* gender. Forming small groups is also an option. Once you decide how you're going to facilitate the discussion, distribute the handout and go for it!

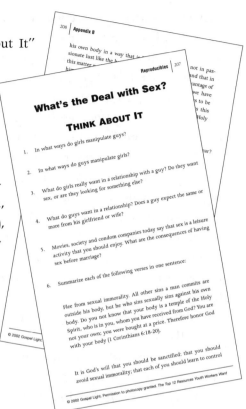

208 | Appendix B

his own body in a way that is
sionate lust like the h...
this matter...
hi...

Reproducibles | 207

not in pas-
and that in
antage of
we have
s to be
s this
Holy

What's the Deal with Sex?

THINK ABOUT IT

1. In what ways do girls manipulate guys?

2. In what ways do guys manipulate girls?

3. What do girls really want in a relationship with a guy? Do they want sex, or are they looking for something else?

4. What do guys want in a relationship? Does a guy expect the same or more from his girlfriend or wife?

5. Movies, society and condom companies today say that sex is a leisure activity that you should enjoy. What are the consequences of having sex before marriage?

6. Summarize each of the following verses in one sentence:

Flee from sexual immorality. All other sins a man commits are outside his body, but he who sins sexually sins against his own body. Do you not know that your body is a temple of the Holy Spirit, who is in you, whom you have received from God? You are not your own; you were bought at a price. Therefore honor God with your body (1 Corinthians 6:18-20).

It is God's will that you should be sanctified: that you should avoid sexual immorality; that each of you should learn to control

© 2002 Gospel Light. Permission to photocopy granted. *The Top 12 Resources Youth Workers Want*

© 2002 Gospel Light

WRAP-UP

Explain: Sex is a great thing—if used the way God intended it. Many think that people should be free to have sex any time and any way they want. These people don't understand that God has a specific plan for sex. Those people say things like "If I'm in love with someone, what better way to express it than to make love?" "Is God so stingy and mean that He would deprive us of something so good?" "Why do there have to be rules? Rules are no fun!"

Conclude with the following example (or adjust the story to fit your situation—if you don't drive a minivan, then obviously this story won't fit!)

I drive a minivan, not exactly a glamorous ride! I mean, what is a minivan good for anyway? It's good for loading up your 2.6 kids and your dog, backing out of your garage and closing your automatic garage door as you pass your white picket fence and scoot down the road to the grocery store. After you exit the grocery store you load your groceries into the rear of the vehicle, load your children back into the van, making sure that all safety restraints have been firmly fastened, and you drive carefully back home. Then you open the automatic garage door, pull in smoothly, stop, unload the groceries, kids and dog, close the garage door and proceed back into your house to resume your life. That's what a minivan is for.

Let's say I'm driving my minivan down the street, and on the other side of the curb I notice a steep embankment descending a rocky path to a muddy field. This is one of those off-road areas that attracts four-wheel-drive vehicles from all over.

Now let's say I think, *Hey, I want to go four-wheeling!* So I yank the steering wheel to the right, swerving off the road, hitting the curb and dropping down the rocky path toward the bottom. As the car bounces down the hill, raising dust and debris the whole way, my front fender hits some rocks and falls off, getting dragged underneath the car. The mirror hits a branch and hangs loosely, and the car starts to slide sideways, finally flipping the rest of the way down the hill. As the car lands on its side, I crawl out of the broken windshield and look at my car. It's crumpled up like a raisin. Its bumper is gone, both mirrors are broken off, only one window remains, and the driveshaft has fallen off.

People who saw me swerve off the road stop and look down the embankment past the settling dust at the crumpled minivan at the bottom of the hill. No doubt they would yell, "Why did you swerve off the road like that?"

I would yell back up to them, "I wanted to go four-wheeling in my minivan!"

They would yell back to me, "You are an idiot!"

I would yell back, "What? Are you saying there are rules for what I can and can't do with my minivan? Can't I drive off a cliff if I want to? Why do there have to be rules about what I can do?"

God has given us a wonderful gift to enjoy—the gift of sex. He gave it to us as an awesome thing that we can share in marriage. It's fun. It feels great. It makes us feel closer to the one we love. But when we abuse this gift—when we use it in a way that it wasn't intended to be used—we will have to face consequences. If you think you can just do whatever you want, you'd better be prepared—your driveshaft just might fall off!

Transition from the funny story by having everyone close their eyes while you share the following word picture:

Picture our world for a minute. You know what the world looks like. There's a lot of craziness around. The list is endless: murders, world hunger, war, sickness, fights, divorce, death and so on. Now, picture this world—this same exact world—with *one* change. Picture that *everyone* in the world believes and follows God's plan for marriage. In other words, everyone finds that one special person they want to spend the rest of their life with, waits until marriage to have sex and enjoys that relationship for the rest of their lives. Imagine you live in this world. What would this one difference make?

Pause and let students share some of their ideas of what such a world would be like. Then continue:

First of all, divorce would not exist. Why? Because everyone is following God's plan for marriage. Moms and dads would stay together, raising their families—no stepparents, no fatherless children.

There would be no prostitution. Why? Because husbands are committed to their wives and wives are committed to their husbands. Since they would follow God's plan for their marriages, they would enjoy good sex lives.

There would be no pornography. Why? Because married people are committed to their relationships and to God's plan for their marriage, and single people are committed to fulfilling God's plan for their lives, so they're saving themselves for marriage.

There would be no sexual abuse of any kind: no child abuse, no molestation, no rapes—nothing! Why? For the same reasons there isn't any pornography or prostitution! Because everyone is committed to following God's will, there is no room for sexual predators.

Abortions would be reduced by at least 90 percent. Why? Because that's at least the percentage of abortions that are performed to terminate pregnancies outside of marriage.

Sexually transmitted diseases wouldn't exist. AIDS, syphilis, gonorrhea, chlamydia (the number one cause of sterility in women), the papilloma virus (the number one cause of cervical cancer in women)—every single sexually transmitted disease would be wiped off the face of the earth.

All of these things—and this isn't even everything that would be different—would happen because of *one* change: People would be following God's plan for marriage.

Invite students to open their eyes and then conclude: **Does God's way sound so bad? Perhaps God knows what He's doing, and we don't. A lot of us are trying to do things our own way, and we end up getting hurt. Then we wonder why. The reason is simply this: God's way is the best way!**

CLOSING PRAYER

Thank God for bringing everyone who attended today's meeting. Thank Him for the wonderful gifts He has given to each of us and seek His help in living life the way He designed it. Pray that God will give everyone a wonderful and safe week.

Program Agenda Nine

HAPPY VALENTINE'S DAY!

TOPIC

Premarital sex

MAIN POINT

Engaging in sex before marriage has harsh consequences; those consequences can be avoided by following God's plan for us.

KEY VERSES

"May your fountain be blessed, and may you rejoice in the wife of your youth. A loving doe, a graceful deer—may her breasts satisfy you always, may you ever be captivated by her love. Why be captivated, my son, by an adulteress? Why embrace the bosom of another man's wife? For a man's ways are in full view of the LORD, and he examines all his paths. The evil deeds of a wicked man ensnare him; the cords of his sin hold him fast. He will die for lack of discipline, led astray by his own great folly." Proverbs 5:18-23.

SUPPLIES

❑ Props for games
❑ Two large pieces of newsprint taped to the wall
❑ Two felt-tip pens
❑ Eight copies of "It Was *Nothing*!" (pp. 209-210)

STUDENTS ARRIVE

• Make everyone feel welcome.
• Learn names and interests of newcomers.
• Give each newcomer a Basic Info Card (see p. 205).

Bring It Together

About 15 minutes after start time, welcome students and start the program.

Introduce New People

Distribute candy to the newcomers and welcome them to the group.

Youth Challenge

Choose an up-front game. Invite two students to volunteer and challenge one another. (Some examples are: Soda Slam, Surgical Glove Blowup and Joust.) Be creative!

Announcements

Announce upcoming activities and events and honor birthdays.

Game

Love Letter Game

> **On a Personal Note:** Kudos to Bryan Carlson from Youth for Christ in Lincoln, Nebraska, for submitting the ideas for this agenda's game and discussion starter to the *YFC JV Newsletter.* —JM

The object of this game is to see who can write the best love letter—the guys or the girls. Divide the group into two teams (guys versus girls, of course!).

While you're lining up each team single file, have staff members write "Honey, I love you so much that . . ." on each team's piece of newsprint. After the teams are lined up, give each team a felt-tip pen.

> **Note:** Warn players *before* they begin that they will be disqualified if they write anything inappropriate. Make sure your leaders keep an eye out for this too.

Starting with the first person in line, players will come forward one at a time and add one word to their team's love letter. After they add their word, they give the felt-tip pen to the next person in line and move to the back of the line. There is NO talking or sharing ideas during the game.

Give teams about four minutes to finish their love letters; then pick one player from each team to read their team's letter aloud. A panel of leaders can vote on the best love letter.

Time permitting, you can play again, this time writing a breakup letter (e.g., "Honey, I know we've had good times, but. . .").

DISCUSSION STARTER

Ask for eight volunteers to perform an impromptu skit. Give each a copy of "It Was *Nothing*!" and assign each a role to play. This is a great skit that demonstrates some of the emotional consequences of giving yourself away too soon. After the skit, move on to the discussion questions:

1. What do you think of this skit?
2. How would you feel if you were Anna?
3. How would you feel if you were John?
4. Do you expect anything of your future spouse?
5. Should your future spouse expect anything of you?
6. If you give yourself away to people before you're married, what do you have left at the altar?

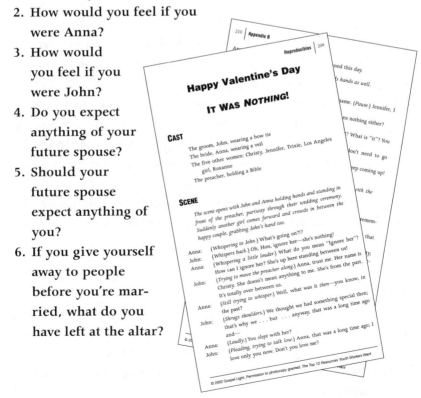

WRAP-UP

Share the following scenario:

> Suppose you have a rich uncle who likes you very much. On your 13th birthday he announces that he will give you $1,000 on your 16th birthday! You spend the next three years thinking about what you are going to do with all that money. On your 16th birthday, your uncle shows up and makes good on his promise. "The money is yours," he says. "You can do whatever you want with it." Then he pauses and holds up his hand. "But I want to teach you to plan for your future, so I'm going to make you another promise. Whatever you have left on your 21st birthday, I will give you that amount *every month* for the rest of your life."
>
> You now have a tough choice: Have some thrills and enjoyment from your money now, or wait five years for a bigger prize that will last a lifetime.

Conclude: What would you do? Very likely, as hard as it would be, you would say, "Hey, I'm going to put off the thrill of spending this money now so that I can enjoy it the rest of my life." That's the way it is with sex. Saving sex for marriage is not saying no to sex. It's postponing it so you can enjoy it to the fullest and over the longest period of time. It's knowing that you will be rewarded more in the future if you wait and that when the future comes you will be very glad that you waited.

Extend a challenge to all in the room to remain pure until marriage. You may consider handing out purity-commitment cards for them to sign and keep with them.

CLOSING PRAYER

Thank the Lord for His love and His grace and for bringing everyone present to this meeting. Pray that He will guide them and help them maintain the purity He has called them to. Pray that every person here (including the leaders) will always seek God's will. Ask for a safe and wonderful week in God's presence.

What Movie Clips Can I Use for Discussion Starters?

TOP 10 MOVIE CLIPS TO PROMOTE DISCUSSION

Okay, so a couple of books have been published on this very subject. But I'm going to write this chapter from a little different perspective—mine!

I love film. I studied film in college and have made a few small productions. Anyone who knows me also knows that if they go see a movie with me, they'll be subject to the rundown on who directed it, the director's history and the history of all the actors. I try to keep on top of the stuff that's coming out of Hollywood.

Movies, music and video are powerful media. Students spend an incredible amount of time and money on them and are greatly affected by them.

USE DISCERNMENT

As much as I wish that Hollywood were more responsible, it seems to be going the opposite direction. So, as much as I love film, I have to use discretion when using the medium as a teaching tool.

Every once in a while someone asks about my use of video clips: "How can you justify showing a clip from an R-rated film? When you use them, aren't you endorsing those movies and what they stand for?" So I'll address this right up front.

I wouldn't show most movies to the students I work with—but frankly, an R-rating isn't the line I use. I'm surprised how often Christians make the R-rating—a secular rating system based on secular morals—their determining line. More PG and PG-13 junk exists out there than ever before. Furthermore, almost every sitcom on the four major networks today has more junk than R-rated movies had just 10 years ago. To be totally honest with you, I would rather kids see some movies than most sitcoms on TV today. A movie such as *Saving Private Ryan* is "Captain Kangaroo" compared to your average five minutes of a television series such as *Friends*, *Dawson's Creek* or *Boston Public*.

Many of you may have heard of Al Menconi. Al runs Al Menconi Ministries (www.almenconi.com), which helps parents communicate values to their children. I appreciate his ministry. He personally challenges and encourages me, and I've brought him in to speak to parents at a big event in Sacramento. When Josh McDowell used to get letters of criticism about touring with Petra (remember those days?), Josh let Al Menconi handle the replies. I've consulted with Al every once in a while when I received a letter or e-mail criticizing me for using R-rated movies. Here's what Al had to say about the subject:

> The point I disagree is where he [the critic] arbitrarily says R-rated movies are evil and then states that we shouldn't have anything to do with evil. While I agree that we shouldn't have anything to do with evil, where does Scripture say *Private Ryan* or R-rated movies are evil? The thing that we need to be careful of is adding to Scripture and giving our addition the same credence as Scripture. Doing this only leads to trouble. The classic example is Eve in the Garden of Eden.

In Genesis 3:3, when the serpent was questioning Eve about God's instructions she added to God's Word. Her reply seemed innocent, "God said that we must not eat from the tree in the middle of the Garden, and we must not touch it or we will die." God simply said, "Don't eat from it." He didn't say anything about touching it. What had she done? She ADDED to God's Word just to be safe; but what's wrong with adding a "bonus of goodness"? By doing this she was implying that God's Word wasn't good enough to stand up to Satan's temptations. She had to "help God out" and she made an extra rule just to be safe! You know where that led.

How does Eve's actions relate to your critic's stand on R-rated movies? Scripture is clear on many things we should avoid, but it is silent about movies. I would say that it is a good policy to avoid R-rated movies in the majority of cases, just as you said in your article, but be careful of saying it is a sin to attend R-rated movies. That's adding to God's Word and it can only lead to trouble. Why not simply say we will evaluate each movie on its own merits in light of Philippians 4:8: "And now, dear brothers and sisters, let me say one more thing as I close this letter. Fix your thoughts on what is true and honorable and right. Think about things that are pure and lovely and admirable. Think about things that are excellent and worthy of praise" [NLT]. Doing this will eliminate 99 and 99/100% of R-rated movies. We are not condemning the movie; we are simply evaluating it in light of God's Word. Be careful about making blanket statements and making conclusions Scripture doesn't.

I believe this would be an excellent time to teach your kids how to discern quality entertainment as a whole. They typically don't know. The problem isn't R-rated movies, the problem is most kids don't know what is good. Their parents or youth pastor said to avoid R-rated movies, but they never taught them what is worthwhile. Many PG and PG-13 movies are much worse than many R-rated movies. Often the child's thought is, *It's not R-rated, so it's okay.* Is it really? Someone needs to teach him how to choose quality entertainment. If most kids are asked if a movie was good, their response is often, "It was funny!" or "It was exciting!" or "It was sexy!" or "It had a lot of special effects!" But they can't explain if it was good or not.

If your kids don't have the ability [to discern] quality entertainment, they will forever be subject to the manipulation of the Hollywood marketing machine. As parents and leaders we must see the vast majority of entertainment as "ammunition" aimed at our kids in the Spiritual war of life. It is our responsibility to teach our children how not to be casualties in this battle for their minds. A way you can do this is to bring "their entertainment" into your Sunday school class and help them filter it through the grid of God's Word just like you did with *Private Ryan*.

Finally, as a caution, study Ephesians 5:1-12. We are to expose evil, but to stay innocent of sin. How can we do that? This is my most difficult challenge as a speaker. My problem is not knowing my material; it's how do I expose evil and still keep my audience innocent of sin. I'm sure you have seen "presentations" on the evils of entertainment that exposed too much. Don't be one of them![1]

Al makes an important point about discretion. I know that he makes me think about some of the stuff I've justified watching. So be careful. My movie suggestions take small clips from movies to promote discussion. I recommend using discretion when choosing which movies to watch.

Now realize, my background is working with unchurched kids in campus clubs. Most of the students I work with are allowed to watch R-rated movies and are always talking about them. In fact, in my recent survey of junior highers (ages 12 to 14), their favorite movie was an R-rated film. For example, in the year 2000 over 90 percent of the students I surveyed had seen *The Matrix* and were talking about it, so we did a discussion on it (see it later in this chapter). Finding clips from such films and discussing them can be advantageous. You have to take precautions and prayerfully consider the possible ramifications. But I don't have a problem with showing clips from some of these movies, especially from a war movie like *Saving Private Ryan*.

As much as I love movies, I have three kids and they don't watch anything but a little public television and films appropriate for kids (*Milo and Otis, Tarzan*, etc.). Websites like screenit.com have been a great help in discerning what is appropriate for viewing. Just because I personally like movies and watch almost no TV, I'm not going to impose that on anyone else. I'm hoping and praying that youth workers out there are going to stay connected to Christ and let their wisdom and decision making flow from Him. Meanwhile, I'll try to keep providing good ideas and resources that may be useful to some and maybe not to others.

As I always say, let's not waste time. Here's a bunch of great video clips (listed alphabetically) that you can use to promote discussion.

> **Note:** The reproducible pages listed in the following movie discussions can be found in appendix *B* at the back of the book.

Note

1. Al Menconi (http://www.thesourcefym.com/videoclips/r-moviesbyal.asp), accessed May 30, 2002.

AMISTAD

In today's polytheistic society it's hard to find good movie clips that portray the truth, especially about Jesus. Most movies and commercials portray a very old or a very stupid, uncaring God. Well, I found another great clip out there that shares the gospel message, if you're tired of using Michael W. Smith's "Secret Ambition" video and *The Jesus Film*. It is Steven Spielberg's film *Amistad* (Dreamworks, 1997), which lost to *Titanic* for Best Cinematography and Best Supporting Actor. So many people were watching the sinking ship that they missed this incredible film.

In the story of *Amistad*, a group of African slaves are in an American jail, awaiting a court decision deciding their fate. One of the characters in the movie, Yamba, starts reading a Bible and is curious about Jesus. This moving scene is intercut with a scene of one of the white men in the film going to a church to pray.

> Cue the movie about 36 minutes from the opening graphic to the scene in which Yamba is in jail looking through a Bible, illustrated with drawings of biblical events. The line that you'll want to begin with is when Yamba's fellow slave is saying, "You don't have to pretend to be interested in that. Nobody's watching but me." Be prepared to end the clip after Yamba says, "This is where the soul goes when you die here. This is where we're going when they kill us. It doesn't look so bad."

Prior to showing the clip, divide students into small groups and give each small group a copy of the discussion starter for the movie (pp. 211-212) and something to write with.

> **Note:** The questions on the discussion starter were designed for an unchurched audience, but they can easily be tweaked and possibly deepened for churched kids.

After showing the clip, ask: **Was Yamba's friend right? Is this just a story? Or does Jesus' life have an effect on us today?** (Here's a great opportunity to present the gospel, or for a more advanced audience, present the Liar, Lunatic or Lord theory (see Josh McDowell's *More Than a Carpenter*[1], Paul Little's *Know Why You Believe*[2], or *Mere Christianity*[3] by C.S. Lewis). Don't pass up the chance to extend an invitation for kids to accept Christ!

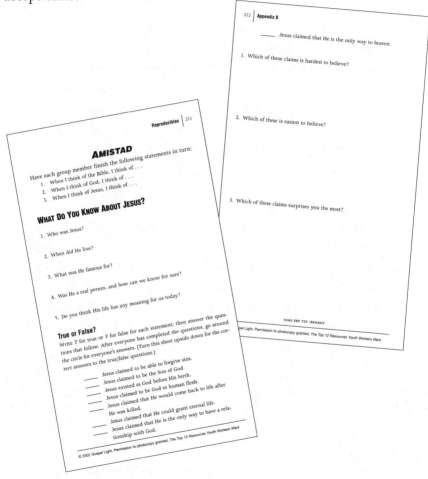

Notes

1. Josh McDowell, *More Than a Carpenter* (Wheaton, IL: Tyndale House Publishers, 1977).

2. Paul Little, *Know Why You Believe* (Wheaton, IL: Scripture Press Publications, 1967).

3. C.S. Lewis, *Mere Christianity* (London: G. Bles, 1952), n.p.

BABE: PIG IN THE CITY

Many of us remember the talking pig Babe. (I remember years ago trying to explain to my wife why I had rented a movie titled *Babe*!) Well, *Babe: Pig in the City* (Universal, 1998), while not half as good as the first film, has a great example of loving your enemies.

The clip you'll be using is about 45 minutes into the film. Some monkeys take Babe out on the town. Babe wants to find some sheep, and the monkeys convince him that there are sheep behind the fence marked "BEWARE OF DOG!" Instead of sheep, Babe finds a Doberman and a pit bull chained up and biting mad! As Babe runs away, the dogs break free and chase after him. The chase scene is quite entertaining. Babe manages to get away from the Doberman, but the pit bull continues the chase, dragging things behind, with the chain still latched to his collar.

The chase ends as Babe jumps off a small bridge into the water and the pit bull gets tangled in the chain. The dog is dangling off the bridge by the chain until the chain slowly slips and the dog starts to drown. Babe, now safe, watches the struggling animal. Moved with compassion for the animal that had just been chasing him, Babe jumps into the water and saves the dog.

Babe's brave feat earns him the respect of all the animals. In the next scene, Babe, again showing mercy, distributes food to all the hungry street animals gathered around.

After showing the clip, have students form small groups and give everyone a copy of the discussion starter for the movie (p. 213).

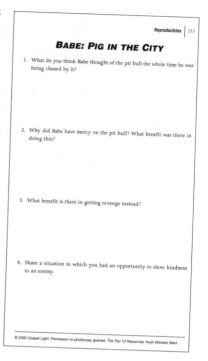

Allow a few minutes for the groups to discuss the questions, and then read the following Scripture passages. (Another option is to assign different groups different passages and have them summarize their assigned verses at the end for the entire group. Hey, I'm flexible; you can be too!)

- Matthew 5:7—"Blessed are the merciful, for they will be shown mercy."
- Matthew 5:23-24—"Therefore, if you are offering your gift at the altar and there remember that your brother has something against you, leave your gift there in front of the altar. First go and be reconciled to your brother; then come and offer your gift."
- Matthew 6:14-15—"For if you forgive men when they sin against you, your heavenly Father will also forgive you. But if you do not forgive men their sins, your Father will not forgive your sins."
- Matthew 18:21-35—The story of the unmerciful servant, ending with, "This is how my heavenly Father will treat each of you unless you forgive your brother from your heart."
- Mark 11:25—"And when you stand praying, if you hold anything against anyone, forgive him, so that your Father in heaven may forgive you your sins."
- Luke 17:3-4—"So watch yourselves. If your brother sins, rebuke him, and if he repents, forgive him. If he sins against you seven times in a day, and seven times comes back to you and says, 'I repent,' forgive him."
- Colossians 3:12-14—"Therefore, as God's chosen people, holy and dearly loved, clothe yourselves with compassion, kindness, humility, gentleness and patience. Bear with each other

and forgive whatever grievances you may have against one another. Forgive as the Lord forgave you. And over all these virtues put on love, which binds them all together in perfect unity."

- James 2:12-13—"Speak and act as those who are going to be judged by the law that gives freedom, because judgment without mercy will be shown to anyone who has not been merciful. Mercy triumphs over judgment!"

CITY SLICKERS

This entire movie (Columbia, 1991) raises questions about what is the one important thing in life.

A great scene is about 59 minutes into the movie in which Curly (played by Jack Palance) takes Mitch (played by Billy Crystal) alone with him to catch a few strays from the herd. After the first night, they end up talking to each other. Start the scene when Curly says, "A cowboy leads a different kind of life . . . " Curly talks to Mitch about life and says it's about one thing. What that one thing is you have to find out for yourself. Mitch spends the rest of the movie looking for that one thing. The movie brings up questions that promote a great discussion. This scene has two cuss words, so you'll have to figure out how to handle that, but the discussion is great.

After showing the clip, have students brainstorm and tell you what their personal one thing is (e.g., family, friends, money, sports, etc.). Then have someone give their testimony about how their quest for all those things didn't bring happiness and how they realized that making God their one thing is the best way to live.

Give everyone a piece of paper and instruct them to tear it into five pieces. Explain: **Material possessions are not the only things that are important to many of us. People, talents and abilities are also of great value. Maybe you like music, baseball, drawing, family and friends. Write down the five most important things in your life on these pieces of paper.** Allow some time for students to write, and then invite them to share what they wrote.

Move into the next activity by having students hold their five papers—representing the five most important things to them—in their hands. Now have them drop any papers on which they have written a material possession because it was stolen. Then have them drop any papers on which they wrote the names of people because those people died. Next, instruct them to drop any papers with physical characteristics or abilities (i.e., beauty, muscles, etc.) because they got a horrible disease that alters their physical health and appearance. Finally, have them drop papers listing a talent or ability because they had an accident and can't do that thing anymore.

Randomly ask students what they have left. Then ask which was the hardest thing to drop. Finally, explain that most cultures believe in life after death. Ask: **Which of these things prepares you for the inevitable conclusion of your life—death?**

Bring a powerful conclusion to the discussion with the following: **During an earthquake, the houses that survive are the ones with solid foundations. We know how solid the foundation of our life is by how we respond during tragedy and tough times. If we crumble, then we have based our lives on a poor foundation. As an example, if what we want in life is money and then we become paralyzed, all the money in the world won't help us be able to walk again.**

Have someone (preferably a student) give a testimony (e.g., "I used to pursue _____ , but I never found happiness. Then I realized that they were temporary, expendable things. God is the only answer to that one thing we search for in our lives"). Have them share how they became a Christian, how God is the most important thing in their life and the difference He has made.

DEEP IMPACT

This movie (Paramount, 1998) is a great discussion starter overall. The whole thing makes you think about what is truly important compared to the trivial temporary stuff we fill our lives with. The movie makes a strong statement about the importance of relationships.

> The first scene to get people thinking starts about an hour and 41 minutes into the movie as Jenny (played by Téa Leoni) pulls her car up to her dad's beach house. Jenny and her father (played by Maximilian Schell) spend these final minutes reconciling and sharing their love, regardless of the barriers they had faced in the past. Another powerful scene takes place moments later as the astronauts on the ship are about to embark on their suicide mission to destroy the other asteroid. This is a strong scene as they take a few moments to say their final good-byes to their loved ones back on Earth.

Set up the meeting room like an airplane, with rows of seats and an aisle down the middle. Use whatever resources you have; a bus would be great, but a room with a bunch of chairs works just as well. Jazz it up as much as you like.

Show the video clip; then announce that you're going to take a plane trip. Have stewardesses bring peanuts, drinks, magazines, etc. After take-off, have the pilot announce trouble and that the plane will be crashing in 10 minutes.

Give each student a piece of paper and a pen so that they can write a letter to their family. Keep announcing how much time they have left to write before the plane crashes. When there's a minute left, have a stewardess come around and collect the letters to put them in a fireproof box, so someone can find them after the crash. Dramatically simulate the crash. Some leaders have actually acquired flight crash simulations, while others have used scenes from old airplane movies.

After the crash, take a few of the letters and, making sure it's OK with the people who wrote them, give them to volunteers to read to the group.

Close the session with this thought: **Did this crash make you think**

---

about things you wish you had done or said? Point out that most of them didn't say that they wished they watched more TV or worked harder at making money—in fact, most probably thought about their relationships, especially the ones they need to work on. **For some of us, the relationship we need to work on the most is our relationship with God.**

THE EMPIRE STRIKES BACK

The Empire Strikes Back (Twentieth Century Fox, 1980) was the first *Star Wars* film to introduce us to Yoda, the Jedi Master. It's a great intro into a discussion about how believing in something means trusting in it and having faith in it.

Cue the movie to the following scene, approximately an hour and eight minutes from the opening graphic. After the huge Imperial Walkers in the snow are defeated, Luke Skywalker (played by Mark Hamill) and R2D2 go to the Dagobah system to meet Yoda and land in a murky swamp. Once Yoda finally reveals himself as the Jedi Master, Luke convinces him that he is ready to begin training. Luke's training consists of exercising, levitating objects and listening to Yoda's insistent chattering!

As Luke is trained in the uses of the Force, his ship sinks deeper in the swamp. Yoda tells Luke he can lift it out with belief in the Force. Doubtful, Luke tries to concentrate and lift the ship out, but he fails due to his lack of belief.

As Luke whines like a two-year-old, little Yoda succeeds in lifting the ship, only for Luke to exclaim, "I don't believe it!"

Yoda replies, "That is why you failed."

Show the video clip; then briefly discuss: **What does it mean to believe in something? Do people's actions reflect their beliefs? If not, do they really believe?**

Share the following story from Tony Campolo:

There was once a great tightrope walker known as The Great Blondin. In the 1800s he strung a tightrope across Niagara Falls, and then, before 10,000 screaming people, inched his way from the Canadian side of the falls to the U.S. side. When he got there, the crowd began shouting his name, "Blondin! Blondin! Blondin!" Finally, Blondin raised his arms to quiet the crowd and shouted, "I am Blondin! Do you believe in me?" The crowd shouted back, "We believe! We believe! We believe!"

Holding up his arms, again he quieted the crowd and shouted, "I'm going back across the tightrope, but this time I'm going to carry someone on my back. Do you believe I can do that?" The crowd yelled, "We believe! We believe!"

Once more, Blondin quieted the crowd. This time he said, "Who will be that person?" The crowd went silent. Nothing. Finally, out of the crowd stepped one man. He climbed on Blondin's shoulders, and for the next three and a half hours, Blondin inched his way back across the tightrope to the Canadian side of the Falls.

Explain: **The whole crowd said that they believed in Blondin, yet only one man truly believed. True belief (or trust) in Christ is a belief of action, not a belief that merely chants, "I believe!"**

Have students form small groups and give everyone a copy of the discussion starter for the movie (p. 214).

FORREST GUMP

I'm sure you remember the 1994 Best Picture (which also won for Best Actor and Best Director), *Forrest Gump* (Paramount, 1994). This movie has a great scene to provoke discussion about prayer and how God's plans are better than ours.

Cue the movie about an hour and 34 minutes from the opening graphic, right after Lieutenant Dan shows up on the dock to become first mate on the shrimping boat owned by Forrest. Continue to the scene where a huge storm comes. **BIG NOTE:** You'll want to do some quick editing or turn off the volume here, where Lieutenant Dan is screaming profanities at God during the storm. End the clip after Forrest's voice says, "After that, shrimping was easy."

After showing the clip, have students form small groups and give everyone a copy of the discussion starter for the movie (p. 215).

Reproducibles | 215

FORREST GUMP

1. Does God listen to all our prayers? Why?

2. Does God answer all our prayers? Why?

3. Why doesn't God answer our prayers in the way we want them answered?

4. How do difficult times (like the storm) make you feel toward God?

5. Why can't we predict or understand God's plans for us?

6. Has there been a time when circumstances in your life were bad, but God used them for good?

© 2002 Gospel Light. Permission to photocopy granted. *The Top 12 Resources Youth Workers Want*

GHOST

This movie (Paramount, 1990) brings up some great discussion questions, such as "What happens to you when you die?"

> If you can edit sections of this film together, it's great to show a couple of the scenes where someone dies (be discerning as some of these scenes are violent). Whenever someone good dies, a little soft light comes and takes them gently away. Whenever someone bad dies, these dark shadowy nasty creatures come and take them away (pretty scary, actually).

After showing the clip, have students form small groups and give everyone a copy of the discussion starter for the movie (p. 216).

Conclude by discussing the many different theories presented by Hollywood about what happens when a person dies: **Some like to believe that there is no life after death; others believe there is an afterlife. Those who believe in heaven or hell often try to create the criteria of who will end up where. Most of us like to convince ourselves that we're OK as long as we don't murder someone and that the little stuff we do doesn't matter. But the truth is that everything we do—big or small—matters.**

216 | Appendix B

GHOST

1. Why do people fear death?

2. How can a person prepare to die?

3. Is death the end of the road? What else is there?

4. Who do you think heaven is for? How do you get there?

5. Who do you think hell is for? How do you get there?

Read Romans 5:8: "But God demonstrates his own love for us in this: While we were still sinners, Christ died for us." Explain: **Even though ALL of us do wrong things—some of us do a lot, some of us do a** little—Christ loved us so much that He took our punishment for us by dying on the cross. Share the following scenario:

> You're out driving one day in your brand new, convertible, turbo-charged, red Camaro. Before you know it, you're going 110 miles per hour. Your moment of fun is disturbed by the sound of a siren. You look into your rearview mirror and see red and blue flashing lights. Gasp! Next thing you know, you're being handcuffed and taken into the police station—no ticket for you; you were going too fast!
>
> When you finally appear before a judge, he looks at the charges and says, "You were going over 100 miles per hour! Do you know what the punishment for that is?" Without pausing to hear your answer, he continues, "It's either $1,000 or six months in jail." Then the judge looks you right in the eye. "Do you have $1,000?" he demands. You desperately search your pockets, hoping for a miracle, but only find $7.33. The judge pronounces you guilty, says "Six months!" and slams his gavel down.
>
> Then something interesting happens. The judge comes down from the bench and takes off his robe. He walks over to you and looks into your eyes again, this time with compassion. "I had to do that as your judge," he begins, "but I don't want you to have to go to jail. So I will go to jail and take your punishment for you."

Explain: Jesus came down from His position as Judge to be our Savior. He paid the price for our sins by dying on the cross. Every sin you ever committed and will commit was paid for on the Cross. He rose again that we may live in a relationship with Him forever. All of our lives are going to come to an unavoidable conclusion someday. The Bible says that we are going to stand before God, but you can have Jesus standing next to you on that day.

Give everyone an opportunity to respond to your message (see the gospel presentation in appendix A on pages 196-203).

THE MATRIX

The blockbuster hit *The Matrix* (Warner Brothers, 1998) with Keanu Reeves was a pretty good film, but it was also extremely violent. You would have to decide which scene you would like to show. I find that most students have seen this film, so you can likely refer to the film without actually showing it.

The film proposes that the world we live in is not real at all; it's just a virtual world that a bunch of computers are fooling us into believing exists. At one point in the film, we see a huge room filled with every human being alive, each one in a bubble and hooked up to a bunch of hoses and tubes. All the hoses and tubes are connected to a long vertical tube or ventricle. The idea is that it is here that humans actually exist; the world they believe they live in is really just a series of images fed to their brains.

Here's the catch: Some people find out the truth and escape their bubbles. They enter the virtual world to fight the bad guys, breaking all the rules of the virtual world because, well hey, because they know the truth. They can dodge bullets and control their surroundings because they know that none of it is real! They can also use their cell phones to call someone outside the virtual world for guidance when it is hard for them to see what is really going on.

We as Christians know the truth: All of this junk (status, money, power, jobs, CD collections, etc.) doesn't matter! Because we know the truth, we don't have to worry about things that come at us: pressures, stress, even actual harm. Jesus says in Luke 12:4-5: "I tell you, my friends, do not be afraid of those who kill the body and after that can do no more. But I will show you whom you should fear: Fear him who, after the killing of the body, has power to throw you into hell. Yes, I tell you, fear him."

You see, as Christians, we can dodge so-called bullets because we know they can't really hurt us—at least not in a way that is eternal. We can also ask for guidance at any time we don't understand what is going on around us. We can pray or read God's Word, and He will guide us through any worldly situation. The only important thing is that which is eternal. There are only two types of things in this world: that which is temporary and that which is eternal. Our mind should be on the eternal—on Christ.

A great clip that I like to show is the scene about an hour and three minutes into the film where you see Cypher (played by Joe Pantoliano) betraying the Freedom Fighters. Cypher is sitting at the dinner table with Agent Smith (played by Hugo Weaving), talking about how he would rather believe in the virtual world. He makes the point that he'd rather have the temporary high, even though he knows it is all a big lie. He says, "You know, I know this steak doesn't exist. I know that when I put it in my mouth, the Matrix is telling my brain that it is juicy and delicious. After nine years, you know what I realize? [He takes a bite of steak.] Ignorance is bliss."

Challenge students to consider what's important: **What do you want to live for? Temporary pleasures that don't last or eternal truth?**

Share the story of the house on the rock from Matthew 7 and conclude: **If you build your life on the rock—a permanent relationship with God—nothing can knock it down.**

A SIMPLE PLAN

Billy Bob Thornton was nominated for Best Supporting Actor in 1998 for his performance in *A Simple Plan* (Paramount, 1998). This is a thought-provoking film that looks at ordinary people faced with extraordinary decisions. The film clearly demonstrates that choices have consequences and that even the simplest of plans can turn into complex disasters.

It's the story of three men, Hank Mitchell (played by Bill Paxton), his brother Jacob (played by Billy Bob Thornton) and Jacob's friend Lou (played by Brent Briscoe), and the complications following their discovery of a downed plane containing over four million dollars in cash. (**Note:** The movie is rated R; preview it and use discretion before showing it. You can refer to the 1998 films at www.screenit.com for specific details.)

A great scene to show is about 30 minutes into the film when Hank, a happily married, upstanding member of his community, poses a question to his pregnant wife, Sarah (played by Bridget Fonda): "Let's say you're out walking in the woods and you find a bagful of money. Would you keep it?" When Hank dumps a huge amount of money on the table, the hypothetical question becomes real. What was a clear-cut decision suddenly becomes a moral dilemma. You can stop the clip at that point.

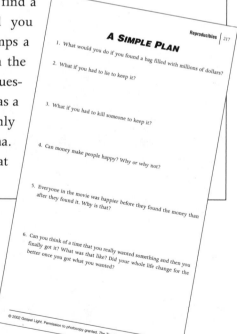

A SIMPLE PLAN   Reproducibles | 217

1. What would you do if you found a bag filled with millions of dollars?

2. What if you had to lie to keep it?

3. What if you had to kill someone to keep it?

4. Can money make people happy? Why or why not?

5. Everyone in the movie was happier before they found it. Why is that?

6. Can you think of a time that you really wanted something and then you finally got it? What was that like? Did your whole life change for the better once you got what you wanted?

After showing the video clip, have students form small groups and give everyone a copy of the discussion starter for the movie (p. 217).

Share Matthew 6:19-21: "Do not store up for yourselves

treasures on earth, where moth and rust destroy, and where thieves break in and steal. But store up for yourselves treasures in heaven, where moth and rust do not destroy, and where thieves do not break in and steal. For where your treasure is, there your heart will be also."

STEPMOM

The movie *Stepmom* (Columbia Pictures, 1998) could be looked at many ways. (**Warning:** If you haven't seen it, be careful reading further as I'm going to spoil some of the key plot changes in the movie!) Some may see it as a film that condones or puts its stamp of approval on the typical American split family. Others may see it for its portrayal of a family's struggle through losing a loved one to cancer. Let's look at the film from yet another perspective.

First of all, I recommend the film. It's fun, it keeps your interest and it might even cause your average ironworker to grab a few tissues throughout the film. Not only is it good—good story, great performances—but it accurately portrays the pain caused by divorce. Sure, some might say that the film's point was to justify the split family, but you can't ignore the tough issues presented in the film that *hurt*!

A great scene to use is about 16 minutes into the film. In this scene, the father (played by Ed Harris) is trying to justify to his two kids, Anna (played by Jena Malone) and Ben (played by Liam Aiken), why he is living with Isabel (played by Julia Roberts).

You could kick off a host of discussions with this scene. If I were doing it, I wouldn't even try to make a point about any issues. I would just state the facts: **Sometimes things happen in our families or at home that hurt. Sometimes Dad leaves or hurts us; sometimes Mom does. Regardless, there's only one person that will never hurt you and will always be there for you when you need Him.**

Tell a *rehearsed* modern-day story of the prodigal son (see Luke 15:11-32). Conclude by explaining that the story you just shared was a modern retelling of a story Jesus told in the Bible: **Jesus tells this story so that we can glimpse what God is like. He is a loving Father who knows your whole past, but loves you, forgives you and wants to be in a relationship with you. He truly cares about your future. He's waiting for each one of us with His arms wide open, waiting to say, "Welcome home, My son. Welcome home, My daughter."**

Do You Have Any Good Event Ideas?

CREATIVE EVENTS AND ACTIVITIES (WHEN BOWLING JUST WON'T CUT IT)

Are the students you work with sick of the same ol' miniature golf on Friday night? Is bowling the best activity available? Well, this chapter is dedicated to giving you some creative event and activity ideas your students will love! You'll notice that I've included some reproducible lists for some of the scavenger-hunt games. Feel free to use the ones I've put together, or make up some lists of your own!

Bananarama

This is a scavenger hunt in which each team is given a banana and a list of things to measure in banana lengths. The cool thing about this hunt is that you don't even need transportation. Everyone can go out on foot.

Sample Items to Measure

(You'll want to provide much more!)

- The height of a stop sign
- A garage door (length and width)
- The length of a Chevy
- The height of a staff person
- The width of a sidewalk
- Someone's waist
- The banana area of a window (i.e., height times width of the window in square bananas!)

Bigger and Better Hunt

This is a scavenger hunt in which each team is sent out with a coat hanger (or similar small item) and told to go door-to-door in the neighborhood asking people if they will trade the coat hanger for something bigger (strictly the size) or better (quality, value, etc.). In the end each team comes back with one item and judges determine the winning team based on who has the biggest or best item.

Simple Rules

- Teams must trade each item they receive for the next item.
- No money or anything else can be offered on the side.
- Team members must stay together.

> **On a Personal Note:** Have some trucks or trailers available for this scavenger hunt. My last Bigger and Better Hunt dump run consisted of an old broken treadmill, a rowboat, a couch and a pair of skis! Be prepared to take a load or two to the dump or thrift store afterwards. —JM

BROOM HOCKEY

Reserve your nearby ice rink and play hockey wearing only tennis shoes and helmets (clothes are good too!). Use brooms as sticks, a small ball as a puck and take out a huge insurance liability policy.

DISPOSABLE CAMERA RALLY

This is a crazy scavenger hunt in which each team has a disposable camera and a vehicle to get around town in (I recommend adult drivers). Give each team a list of items worth different points to take pictures of. (See page 218 for a reproducible list.) You can develop the pictures at a one-hour place—or use digital cameras—and see results that evening or develop them for a PowerPoint slide presentation (many places will develop pictures on CD) the next week. The options are endless! This can be a great game for an all-nighter too.

(See page 218 for a reproducible list.)

218 | Appendix B

DISPOSABLE CAMERA RALLY

MANDATORY PICTURES
Must have pictures of all of the following to qualify:
- ☐ The entire team making faces at the camera
- ☐ Two team members eating the same piece of licorice
- ☐ Someone in the group lying down in a bed
- ☐ The entire team standing on their heads

1,000 POINT PICTURES
- ☐ A team member feeding a stranger
- ☐ A lady holding a child's hand
- ☐ A guy smoking
- ☐ A gas station attendant washing a window
- ☐ A couple on a park bench
- ☐ Someone ordering Chinese food
- ☐ A lady walking her dog

1,500 POINT PICTURES
- ☐ A person driving a bus
- ☐ A firefighter in uniform
- ☐ A team member combing someone's hair
- ☐ Someone buying dog food
- ☐ A little kid licking a sucker
- ☐ Someone preaching on a street corner
- ☐ A team member hugging a car salesman

3,000 POINT PICTURES
- ☐ A dog relieving itself
- ☐ A couple on a bicycle built for two
- ☐ A team member helping an elderly person across the street
- ☐ A police car with its lights flashing
- ☐ Someone walking past a sign that says something like "Do Not Enter" or "Do Not Pass"
- ☐ The entire team on a boat

© 2002 Gospel Light. Permission to photocopy granted. The Top 12 Resources Youth Workers Want

DIVE-IN MOVIE

We did this event on Discovery Channel's Shark Week and someone e-mailed me the same idea that same week, so it must be a good one! You can do as we did and barbecue thresher shark and advertise it as the event where you eat the shark!

Set up a video projection unit to project the movie *Jaws* onto a huge screen at the edge of a swimming pool. Have everyone bring their air mattresses or inner tubes. (I got a big river raft from my friends at Rock 'n' Water, the best white-water rafting camp in California. Check them out on my link page.) Turn all the lights off except the pool lights and have everyone float in the water while watching the movie. During the middle of the movie have some of the guys swimming around acting like sharks and scaring people. The sky's the limit with this one, folks. Enjoy!

Five-Buck Receipt Rush

This event requires little planning and is always really fun. Sometimes it also requires a little of your budget, depending on how many kids are on each team. I usually charge a dollar and end up in the red (losing money). If you charge two bucks you could break even or even come out ahead. I advertise that the winning team gets pizza at our local cheap, cardboard-tastin' pizza joint.

Form as many teams as you have vehicles and seatbelts. Each team is given $5 to spend as they wish. The contest, however, is to get the most receipts, each from a different store or restaurant. The total dollar amount of these receipts must be less than $5. The team that gets the most receipts and makes it to the meeting spot (the pizza place) by a certain time is the winner.

I also have a rule that every receipt given must be witnessed by a staff member and signed by them. This keeps the team together and prevents them from whipping out a receipt they had from the day before.

If I do have extra money left over, I sometimes surprise them and buy them all sodas. This helps to appease the losing teams a little.

Gym Hockey

Somehow acquire some hockey sticks and access to a gym. Rotate teams for a night of fun competition.

Manhunt

This is a great event to market your group and increase group size. This works best if your group has already been meeting for a few weeks and has built a little bit of momentum (see chapter 8).

> **On a Personal Note:** I like to do this event a week or two before our kickoff. This way I can pump the kickoff (usually a Pizza Bash or Burger Bash) to all the new faces! —JM

Advertise a Manhunt, but don't tell anyone what it is. Have enough transportation available for twice the number of students that you normally have (the crowd will be growing as the event progresses!). Divide everyone into teams and let them know that this is a contest to bring back as many of their friends as possible to the meeting place by a given time (usually a little over an hour). Give each team a list and send them out in half-empty vehicles to find friends who match the descriptions on the list. (See page 219 for a reproducible list.)

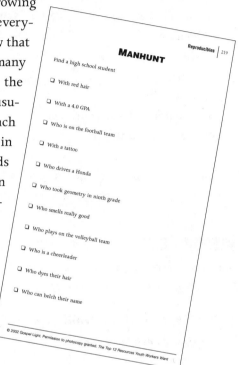

When everyone returns, have some fun games and activities, along with a brief promotion of what your group is like, and invite everyone back. Give the winning team, guests and all, some cool prizes.

MARATHON MADNESS

This is the age-ol' all-nighter. Some people call it a "lock-in," but I don't, because we don't stay in one place. I've done a lot of these all-nighters and they are always a hit!

This event requires enough vehicles to haul your entire group around, enough drivers who can handle driving all night and enough coffee to help keep the drivers awake! Start at your usual facility with some fun organized games. After a couple of hours, switch to a new location. Keep switching locations every few hours for an all-night marathon of activities. Here's your opportunity to do the proverbial bowling, roller skating, broom hockey, etc.

This does take some logistical planning ahead, but it's worth it. Sacramento Youth for Christ does an event like this with a lot of area churches and has had 1,400 students participate! With a group that large, you have to rotate different groups to different places at the same time.

Possible Locations and Activities

- Movie—at your meeting location, someone's house or outside
- Swimming
- Bowling
- Laser tag
- Roller skating
- Teen center or local youth center
- Racquetball/tennis club

A fun conclusion is to end up somewhere for breakfast. What a great opportunity for your pastor to serve pancakes to everyone!

MELON FEST

Sometimes a big event can be a collection of games with the same theme. This is a great one, where the theme is *melons*!

Watermelon Helmet Contest

That's right, have each team carve a helmet (or helmets) out of watermelons. You can go for the gladiator look or more of the Darth Vader look. Team members must wear their helmets throughout the event.

Watermelon Seed-Spitting Contest

Need I explain?

Cantaloupe Bowling

Create an alley in the parking lot and set up 10 2-liter soda bottles at the end of the alley. Leave the bottles full and give a bonus if someone busts them open.

Melon Armor

Give each team a ball of string, a roll of duct tape, a knife and about five melons of different varieties. Have each team dress one of their team members in *full melon armor*. That's right, dress up this person in as much armor, made of melons, as humanly possible. (You may want to make the armored team member a guy!)

Watermelon Toss

You guessed it! Get your strongest guys to do a take-off on the age-old egg toss. Teammates line up facing each other; one tosses the watermelon to the other; then both take a step back and continue backing up after each toss. It *can't* hit the ground. The last pair still tossing wins!

Seedless Watermelon-Eating Contest

Bring two representatives from each team up front, an Eater and a Cutter. At "Go," the Cutter starts cutting watermelon for the Eater to eat. The Eater scarfs as many watermelons down as possible within a given period of time.

Ultimate Cantaloupe

This is just like Ultimate Frisbee but with a cantaloupe! Form two teams, each trying to get to the opposing end zone. Instead of a kickoff, just have one team start on its side of the field. Teams work their way down the field, passing the melon to each other until they score.

Rules

- When a player catches the cantaloupe, they can take only three steps and then they must toss it.
- Unlike Ultimate Frisbee, in which you can knock the Frisbee out of the air, there is no knocking the melon down. If it is knocked out of play, possession returns to the opposite team of the last person who touched the melon before it hit the ground.
- Defensive players must give opponents who are holding the melon at least three feet of space around them.
- If no one catches a toss and the melon drops to the ground (without being touched), possession goes to the opposite team.
- As an added twist, if one team busts the cantaloupe, the other team automatically scores. Have extra cantaloupes available.

Bobbing for Melons

This game requires a pool or some other large body of water. You can play this many ways: One way is to fill a pool with all kinds of melons, even a few vegetables of choice (cucumbers, squash, etc.), and give a team a certain amount of time to retrieve the produce. You can increase the degree of difficulty by doing this activity at night with no lights or by putting Vaseline all over the produce.

Steal the Melon

That's right, this is like good ol' Steal the Bacon *except* with a greased watermelon in the center. Line up two teams facing each other, number team members off and call out a number. The players with that number have to grab the watermelon and get it back to their side.

MEMOREX MADNESS

This is a scavenger hunt where sounds are the items to be found. Teams with tape recorders set out to record a list of items worth various points. (See page 220 for a reproducible list.)

SLEDGE-O-MATIC SMASHOFF

This is a messy one, so make sure everyone knows to wear grubbies!

Make sledges out of a block of wood and a sledge handle (short 2x4s nailed together will also work). The idea is to bring out tons of messy objects and smash them in front of the audience, just like the comedian Gallagher has been doing for years.

---

220 | Appendix B

MEMOREX MADNESS

Record the following sounds:

❑ A baby crying

❑ A toilet flushing

❑ A siren

❑ A burp

❑ A lion's roar

❑ Someone singing out of tune

❑ A jet taking off

❑ A Kmart intercom announcement

❑ A used-car commercial

❑ Someone arguing

❑ A church organ

❑ Someone swimming

❑ A dog barking

© 2002 Gospel Light. Permission to photocopy granted. The Top 12 Resources Youth Workers Want

---

> **On a Personal Note:** You can be creative and have various messy activities to go along with this one. Some great ideas are Jell-O Wrestling and Shaving Cream Beauty Parlor. You might consider finishing with Water Wars! —JM

Good Items to Smash

- Gallons of milk
- Gallons of chocolate milk
- Cartons of orange juice
- Watermelons
- Various fruits
- Heads of lettuce
- Yogurt cups
- Cottage cheese
- Bags of flour
- Containers of syrup
- Bottles of canola oil

Bad Items to Smash

- Anything in a can (we once sent a can flying at about 70 mph into a girl's shin! Ouch!)
- Anything in a glass container (duh!)

STAFF HUNT

Have one of your staff members dress in an unrecognizable getup and hide somewhere in a local mall. You can give clues if you want, or you can just turn the kids loose to find the person.

> **On a Personal Note:** Warn the kids to pretend that they are shoppers so that they don't get kicked out of the mall. Did I just say that out loud? Did I just tell you to lie? Forget that hint! Instead, tell them to be calm and not to run around like imbeciles! —JM

VIDEO SCAVENGER HUNT

This one's a scavenger hunt where each team has a video camera and a list of items to film. (See pages 221-222 for a reproducible list.)

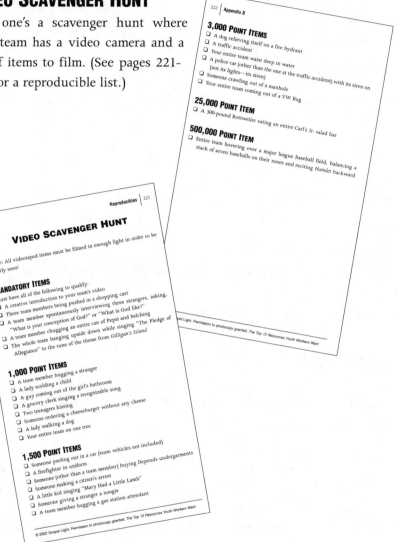

3,000 POINT ITEMS
- ❑ A dog relieving itself on a fire hydrant
- ❑ A traffic accident
- ❑ Your entire team waist deep in water
- ❑ A police car (other than the one at the traffic accident) with its siren on (not its lights—its siren)
- ❑ Someone crawling out of a manhole
- ❑ Your entire team coming out of a VW Bug

25,000 POINT ITEM
- ❑ A 300-pound Rottweiler eating an entire Carl's Jr. salad bar

500,000 POINT ITEM
- ❑ Entire team hovering over a major league baseball field, balancing a stack of seven baseballs on their noses and reciting *Hamlet* backward

VIDEO SCAVENGER HUNT

Note: All videotaped items must be filmed in enough light in order to be clearly seen!

MANDATORY ITEMS
Must have all of the following to qualify:
- ❑ A creative introduction to your team's video
- ❑ Three team members being pushed in a shopping cart
- ❑ A team member spontaneously interviewing three strangers, asking, "What is your conception of God?" or "What is God like?"
- ❑ A team member chugging an entire can of Pepsi and belching
- ❑ The whole team hanging upside down while singing "The Pledge of Allegiance" to the tune of the theme from *Gilligan's Island*

1,000 POINT ITEMS
- ❑ A team member hugging a stranger
- ❑ A lady scolding a child
- ❑ A guy coming out of the girl's bathroom
- ❑ A grocery clerk singing a recognizable song
- ❑ Two teenagers kissing
- ❑ Someone ordering a cheeseburger without any cheese
- ❑ A lady walking a dog
- ❑ Your entire team on one tree

1,500 POINT ITEMS
- ❑ Someone peeling out in a car (team vehicles not included)
- ❑ A firefighter in uniform
- ❑ Someone (other than a team member) buying Depends undergarments
- ❑ Someone making a citizen's arrest
- ❑ A little kid singing "Mary Had a Little Lamb"
- ❑ Someone giving a stranger a noogie
- ❑ A team member hugging a gas station attendant

Do I Really Have to Plan Beyond Next Week?

PLANNING FOR GREATER IMPACT

Every year for my campus ministry snow retreat, I used to rent a great cabin by Donner Lake about two hours away from where I live in Northern California. It had a huge main room where we could have all of our group time, a great kitchen and excellent sleeping arrangements. Best of all, it was always covered with snow.

Problem was, this place started to get popular. I had to start booking it at least six months out. No problem—only a 10-minute phone call in July; who can't do that? Well, every year I had friends in ministry calling me up in November or even December asking if I knew of any cool locations for a January snow retreat. As you know, a weekend retreat is a great time to pull kids out of their world for a few days, build relationships with them and maybe even talk with them about the choices they're making. Sadly, every place is booked by November.

"Oh well, I guess we'll just go up and play in the snow for a day."

A day in the snow? Sure that's fun; it might even bring out some new students. But was that the event you wanted to do? What about getting away with students for a weekend?

Don't Fail to Plan

It's a shame when opportunities for good ministry are missed because someone simply didn't make a phone call in July. It all comes down to planning. People don't plan to fail; they fail to plan!

People don't plan to fail; they fail to plan!

As I was previewing the new edition of *The Youth Builder* by Jim Burns and Mike DeVries, I underlined this statement:

Planning ahead is important. So how do you do it? How do you make sure that you aren't going to miss a 10-minute July phone call? And aren't there more things than one snow weekend to plan?

Every year take just an hour or two—no joke, just an hour or two—and lay out your year's schedule. Start with a blank piece of paper or a blank computer screen and start planning.

> Vision usually isn't the thing that hinders most youth ministries: It's a lack of administration that sinks many of them . . . In reality, a well-administered ministry will provide more valuable time to spend with your students.[1]

On the following page are samples of the reproducible "Jonathan's Ministry Planning Checklist" found on pages 223-225.

Start with a Purpose

The first thing we have to do is remember our purpose. Let's not fall into the category of ministries that plan events, activities, camps and retreats simply because "we've always done it."

What is the purpose of your ministry? Is it biblical? If your purpose is to have the biggest youth group in Plano, Texas, chances are it isn't biblical.

As a campus-outreach minister, my purpose was something like this: "Reach this campus with the life-changing message of Jesus Christ, disciple them and plant students in the local church." You'll notice that this statement mentions three purposes: reach, disciple and plant. Most good purpose statements include several different purposes in them.

There are some excellent training programs that focus on developing your purpose. I could devote this whole chapter to vision statements, mission statements, etc. As valuable as that is, I'm going to assume that you've already done that and that you can simply plug in your mission, your vision or your purpose right on the top of the page.

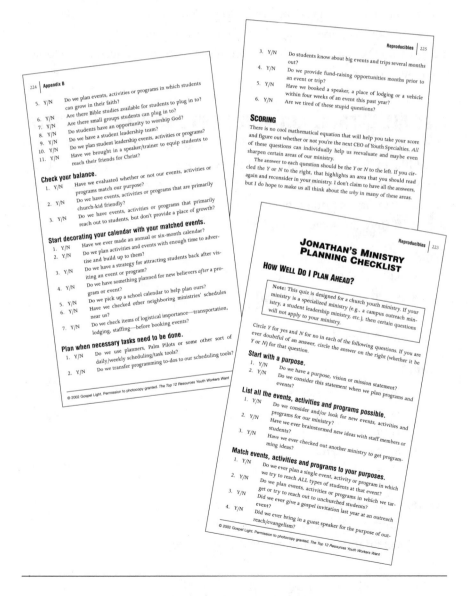

In his book *Purpose-Driven Youth Ministry*, Doug Field gives us an example of a purpose statement from a church in Mesa, Arizona:

> The goal of our student ministry is to expose teenagers to God's love, to equip them to exalt God, to enjoy other believers and to experience the work of the ministry.[2]

This statement from a church I'll call First Church of Mesa values five different purposes: evangelism, discipleship, worship, fellowship and service or ministry—all great basics for any youth group. If you haven't ever put a purpose statement together, I encourage you to do so. As we dig deeper into the planning process, you'll see the importance of developing your purpose.

LIST ALL EVENTS, ACTIVITIES AND PROGRAMS POSSIBLE

Now that your purpose is clear, take the time to brainstorm every event you'd like to do in the upcoming year, every event you did last year, every event the church next door did last year and the events you always wanted to do but haven't done for some reason or other. No joke; just start listing stuff! Here are some examples:

Trips
- Skiing in Utah
- Six Flags amusement park
- Israel
- Rio Linda

Camps
- Woodleaf
- Estes Park
- Hume Lake
- Snow weekend
- Forest Home

Weekly Programs
- Impact—Tuesday-night program
- Celebration—Sunday-morning youth worship

- Soul Xtreme—Student-led campus-outreach club
- Going Deep—Small groups

Mission Trips
- Mexicali
- Salvation Army workday
- Ireland

Activities
- Video Scavenger Hunt
- Christmas banquet
- Concert

Miscellaneous
- Billy Graham Crusade
- Harvest Crusade

You get the idea. Your list should be much longer. If you start out with the previous year's list of events, it's not hard.

MATCH EVENTS, ACTIVITIES AND PROGRAMS TO PURPOSE

Now that you have your purpose statement written down and your list of possible stuff to do, it's time to match activities and events to your purposes. We can't do that unless we really understand how activities can accomplish a given purpose.

A Common Misconception

I don't want to get on my soapbox, but this is the most neglected step I see in youth-ministry planning today. Youth ministries often plan activities, events and even weekly programs without any idea what the purpose behind that particular activity is.

Whenever I'm booked to speak at an event or camp, I always ask "What is the purpose of the event?" Often I get a blank expression or a silence on the other end of the phone. One time this happened, and so I clarified by asking, "Is this an outreach event, a growth event or a leadership event?"

"All three!" came the reply.

That answer always kills me. Let me make a few points:

- There are unbelieving students out there who never ever want to set foot in a church.
- There are unbelieving students who would go to church if there was a good enough reason—like an attractive member of the opposite sex inviting them.
- There are unbelieving students who are curious about spiritual things, might truly be seeking an answer to the emptiness in their lives and realize that the answer might be at church.
- There are lukewarm students who have grown up in the church, heard a thousand messages, but don't make God a priority in their lives.
- There are believing students who have just made a commitment to Christ and are ready to grow.
- There are believing students who are ready to serve and minister to others.

Different events target different kids. Let's face it, if you want to target the kid who never wants to set foot in a church, 99 percent of the time you are *not* going to start by inviting him to a Wednesday-night prayer meeting. However, you may invite him to the skateboard event, the ski retreat or the concert. If you want to provide a place of growth for the students who've just made commitments to Christ, you probably are not going to just take them to outreach events that present the gospel and give an invitation each week. However, you *would* want to bring them to the new-believers' Bible study or the weekly Cross Training growth program.

Don't try to do it all with one event. If you try to target all the above students with all your events, your impact will be weak. That's why different programs, events and activities achieve different strategies of your purpose.

How to Match Events, Activities and Programs

To illustrate how to do this step, we'll look at First Church of Mesa and see how we would match events and activities to each of their purposes. This church might come up with the following five types of events/activities/programs for each area of their purpose statement:

Evangelism

First Church of Mesa would need to have events and activities that reach out to unbelievers inside and outside the church. Remember, these may be events that are just plain fun so that people in Mesa's youth group feel comfortable inviting their friends to come. It's not bad to have an event with the simple goal of bringing in lots of kids and showing them a good time. This will help you do several things:

> **Fun events open the door to evangelism opportunities.**

1. It surrounds you with needy students.

   On hearing this, Jesus said, "It is not the healthy who need a doctor, but the sick. But go and learn what this means: 'I desire mercy, not sacrifice.' For I have not come to call the righteous, but sinners" (Matthew 9:12-13).

2. It gets your students comfortable with asking their friends to church.

   Then, leaving her water jar, the woman went back to the town and said to the people, "Come, see a man who told me everything I ever did. Could this be the Christ?" (John 4:28-29).

3. It puts your staff in the position to build relationships with outreach students.
4. It helps outreach students see opportunities to be involved in more church activities; many of these activities will present the gospel message.

Fun events open the door to evangelism opportunities. Don't underestimate the power of well-trained relational staff spending time with students in order to gain opportunities to share the gospel. This can be as rewarding as an outreach event in which the gospel is preached.

Unfortunately, I've seen groups go overboard with fun events. Week to week there is only fun and games—no depth and no staff building relationships with students. I think most churches would agree that the primary reason they do fun and games is to bring students out and expose them to the life-changing message of Jesus Christ. So don't stop at fun and games; make sure that you also have *evangelism* events that share the gospel message. Here are some ideas for events:

- Back-to-school swim party
- Amusement-park trip
- Weekend retreat where the gospel is presented
- Harvest Crusade or local outreach rally
- A weekly program with the purpose of outreach (see chapter 3 for a bunch of these)

Discipleship

What better purpose to follow evangelism than discipleship? First Church of Mesa does not want to just bring students to Christ and then abandon them. Mesa wants to disciple Christians and help them grow in their faith.

> Therefore, go and make disciples of all the nations, baptizing them in the name of the Father and the Son and the Holy Spirit. Teach these new disciples to obey all the commands I have given you. And be sure of this: I am with you always, even to the end of the age (Matthew 28:19-20, *NLT*).

So First Church of Mesa needs activities, events and programs in which Christian students can grow in their faith. Many youth ministries have this at their weekly program. But realize that retreats, camps and activities can do this just as well.

A friend who's a youth worker in my area always takes his students on a Relationships Retreat. The purpose of this retreat is to talk to Christian students about their relationships with the opposite sex. This is an important part of their growth as young men and women. At this retreat, many of the students pledge to wait for sex until marriage.

Many camps have the purpose of discipleship or growth. It's great for churches to provide a time of fellowship and spiritual growth for Christian students in this atmosphere.

Don't forget about Bible studies or small groups. These are excellent ways for students to grow in their relationships with God as well as with other Christian students. Here are some examples:

- Impact—every Tuesday night (weekly program)
- Bible studies
- Small groups (chapter 10 takes a deeper look at these)
- Relationships retreat
- Winter camp

Worship

First Church of Mesa needs to provide a time of worship for its students, since worship is one of its purposes. We've seen a lot of ministries incorporate this purpose more in the last decade as they've realized the power of the Holy Spirit through worship. Worship bands like Sonic Flood and Delirious? were some of the first bands that made worship songs mainstream. *WOW Worship* CDs are growing more popular each year.

Many students respond well to programs centered around praise and worship. Worship can also be a part of many of the activities and events already planned. For example:

- Celebration—Sunday youth worship service
- Impact—every Tuesday night (worship is part of weekly discipleship/growth program)
- Winter camp—a worship band is brought along to lead worship
- Sitting together as a group in the main church service in order to experience corporate worship

Fellowship

Fellowship is another purpose of First Church of Mesa. This church should include events that provide fellowship among believers.

> They devoted themselves to the apostles' teaching and to the fel-
> lowship, to the breaking of bread and to prayer (Acts 2:42).

I have received some e-mails from people who complain that I shouldn't have all the fun and games on my website. Several have even argued that every game *must* have a biblical application.

I understand that some youth ministries have sacrificed *any* depth for *just* fun and games. However, I'm concerned when people feel that we can't provide students a time of *just* fun.

We must realize that students are bombarded by hundreds of opportunities to make bad decisions each day. Many of these are *very* attractive decisions that result in a lot of pain. One of the best defenses our students have against these tough choices is fellowship. Christian students should build relationships with other Christians so they can encourage each other during tough times.

> Let us not give up meeting together, as some are in the habit of doing, but let us encourage one another—and all the more as you see the Day approaching (Hebrews 10:25).

> Two are better than one, because they have a good return for their work: If one falls down, his friend can help him up. But pity the man who falls and has no one to help him up! Also, if two lie down together, they will keep warm. But how can one keep warm alone? Though one may be overpowered, two can defend themselves. A cord of three strands is not quickly broken (Ecclesiastes 4:9-12).

Don't feel guilty about providing a time for just plain fellowship. Realize that relationships are very important to God. In fact, they are so important that His two greatest commandments concern relationships: "Love God" and "Love others" (see Matthew 22:37-39).

Fellowship is a great purpose, and many of our events can provide that. For example:

- Fun events

- Impact—every Tuesday night (weekly program)
- Bible studies
- Small groups
- Camps
- Retreats

Service/Ministry

Ministry is the fifth purpose of the First Church of Mesa. This church should provide opportunities for students to minister, to serve and maybe even to lead. As students grow in their faith, serving others becomes an incredible part of Christian growth. We can provide many opportunities for students to do this. A leadership team (i.e., where a core group of students help run your ministry) is a great way to achieve this (see chapter 12). Leadership retreats, conferences and training are also very effective. Sometimes the best chance for a student to minister is in the opportunity to share their faith with a friend or bring them to church. Here are some suggestions:

- Core team—monthly leadership meeting
- Student worship team—lead worship, meet for a weekly Bible study and prayer time
- Leadership conferences, such as DC/LA, denominational student leadership conferences, etc.
- Student counseling at an evangelism event
- Mission trips
- Bringing friends to church

As you can see, there are a lot of things we can do with students that do more than just keep them busy. Take time to match your activities, programs and events to your purposes in this way. This keeps you focused, not only on the purpose at hand, but also on the big picture of why you are doing what you do. Moreover it will help you answer questions from angry parents demanding to know why their child threw up after eating SPAM, drinking a gallon of milk and spinning around a bat 10 times!

Check Your Balance

At this point, you've laid out your purpose and listed all possible programs, activities and events and matched them with your purposes. Now you need to check the balance of these activities before filling out the calendar. Here's what I mean by checking the balance.

Are your purposes balanced? Do you have the right amount of programs, activities and events in each purpose area? If the First Church of Mesa has purposes of evangelism, discipleship, worship, fellowship and ministry, does the church's youth calendar have a balanced number of programs, activities and events in each purpose area?

For example, let's say that the First Church of Gehenna has a celebration service on Sunday (worship, discipleship), a weekly Tuesday-night Growing Deep program (discipleship, worship), small groups (fellowship, discipleship), a Bible camp (discipleship, worship, fellowship) and a leadership team that helps run all of these (ministry). Sounds great, right? What is missing? *Evangelism* is missing from this ministry!

This ministry should add monthly fun events to which students can invite their friends or specific outreaches to which they bring in a speaker to share the gospel. Your annual calendar should reflect every aspect of your overall purpose. This should include different types of programs that meet the needs of different students. If the calendar is filled predominantly with a bunch of fun and games and has nothing with discipleship value, chances are that students aren't going to be challenged to grow in their faith. Furthermore, your students who are eager to grow either go somewhere else where they can grow or they stay and become stagnant.

On the other hand, if your calendar is filled with only deep Bible studies, prayer meetings and intense biblical teaching, chances are your ministry won't be doing a lot of evangelism. Students won't feel like they can bring their friends and if they do, their friends will probably not feel comfortable, and they themselves may not come back.

A balanced ministry with a balanced calendar will have programs, activities and events in each purpose area—reaching out to students, providing a place of growth and building mature Christians who will minister to others. Make sure your ministry's schedule is balanced to reflect your purpose.

START DECORATING THE CALENDAR WITH EVENTS

Now that you have in mind what events fulfill what purposes, you can fill out the calendar. Unfortunately, many youth workers often start just filling in events on their calendars. However, you need to make sure the year's events reflect your *biblical* purpose for ministry.

This is the fun step. Lay out your calendar for the school year, grab activities, programs and events from your lists and plop them on your calendar. I wish this step was as easy as simply grabbing and plopping, but obviously there are several things to consider when choosing dates.

Natural Order

No, I'm not talking about some Darwinian principle; I'm talking about the order in which events should be placed on your calendar. For example, don't just plan a huge event at the beginning of the year with no warning. Some ministries have planned big events, passed out flyers and assumed they would get a great response, only to be disappointed with the turnout. Many events like this need a rolling start, a momentum. This kind of planning is described in detail in chapter 9, specifically in the section about creating momentum (p. 152).

Think beyond the event! For example, let's say you spent all of September pumping a huge kickoff event in October. The event turns out fantastic; tons of new students show up and everyone has a great time. The question in any new student's mind is, *Is there a reason to come back?* What can you pump at that event to bring students back the next week? Make sure to communicate what exciting thing you'll be doing next week. Don't feel like you always need to be throwing watermelons in wood chippers or eating goldfish from a vat of apple juice. You can draw people back with speakers and good topics. "Don't miss next week's group. We're going to talk about 'Recommending Sex: What the Bible Actually Says About It!' "

If you have a big outreach event at which students have an opportunity to respond to the gospel, what do you have planned for those students? Do you have mentors who can start discipling those students the next week? Do you have a new believers' Bible study that can start immediately?

Make sure your natural order of events makes sense. Build momentum for events and activities. Have appropriate follow-up programs and events ready to keep that momentum rolling.

Church Calendar

Don't forget to check your church's master calendar. Most churches have more than just youth ministry happening throughout the year. You don't want to plan a retreat when most of your staff wants to be at another major church event the same weekend. Furthermore, you don't want to have any facility conflicts with another group from the church. The last thing a youth pastor needs is to be at war with the choir. (My dad always said when Satan was kicked out of heaven, he landed in the choir loft!)

School Calendar

When planning your youth-ministry calendar, it is also important to consider the calendars of several of the various schools your students attend. I always pick up school calendars to see when activities, events and sports games are scheduled. I'll never forget the year that I planned a great winter retreat, only to find out that it was on the same weekend as a school's winter dance. This retreat was usually one of the greatest outreach events of the year for us. We always saw a large number of kids make decisions for Christ that weekend. That year I lost several needy kids to the dance, which could have been avoided by my checking the school calendar. The same can happen when a weekly youth-group night competes with football games, basketball practice or band concerts. Try to choose a night that doesn't interfere with the schools' sports or music schedule.

Area Churches and Parachurch Organizations

Many of my readers work for parachurch organizations such as Young Life, Youth For Christ/Campus Life or Campus Crusade. Check to see when the local high school or college group meets at area churches. Planning your events in competition with these churches closes two major doors: the ability to plug students in to that group and good rapport with that youth worker.

Facilities, Equipment and Transportation

You can pencil in your week at a camp whenever you want to go—but the camp you want to attend might have only one week in the entire year still available; and that week may not be the week you penciled in! The same with buses, vans and drivers. Make sure these are available on the dates you choose. Many of these logistical hoops might have to be jumped through before penning in a date—which leads us to the last step.

PLAN WHEN TASKS NEED TO BE DONE

Planning a year in advance not only keeps you on track with your ministry focus, it also opens opportunities for excellence in your activities, programs and events. If you plan ahead, you have *10 times* the chance of getting that facility, the transportation and the speaker you want. All of us have been at events in which some of those aspects weren't great. It affects the attitudes of students, the attitudes of staff and very often, the overall perception of the trip.

Money

Let's face it, money is a big issue for many of us. Lots of times we choose against certain trips or events because of the cost. Planning ahead opens doors for fund-raising as well.

Every year that I ran a campus outreach in Sacramento, I took a group of students on a huge trip over Easter break to Southern California. This trip was a week of amusement parks and the beach, including a program every night, and every year a large number of students gave their lives to Christ. This trip cost over $200 per student. For some students that's no big deal, but for most of the kids I worked with it was a huge deal!

I wanted these kids to go, so I started fund-raising opportunities early in the year. We started selling See's candy, and we did workdays during which they solicited hourly pledges to feed the homeless at the Salvation Army. By means of these fund-raisers, I saw students who never could have even considered going, become able to go, and they received Christ on the trip. Why? Because I made a couple of calls to the Salvation Army. I printed out pledge sheets, stopped by See's candy and loaded up my trunk every two weeks. A lot of work? Yes. Kids coming to Christ as a result? Yes. Worth it? Absolutely.

Documentation

Look at the events for the year, one day at a time. Ask yourself, *Is there anything I need to do prior to this month to make this event successful?* If the answer is yes, write it down. For example, do you have an event that is going to need a guest speaker? Why not start looking for one now? (In fact, check out www.thesourcefym.com/speakers/to begin your search!)

Every year I would plan a guest speaker within the first month or so to come in and share the gospel. At the school I worked with, rap music was very popular, so I would usually book a Christian rap artist. This had to be done months ahead of time. I often had to book an extra-large sound system for this event. Several years in a row I contacted a local church that sent several guys to come out, set up and run the sound for the concert. These guys, excited about what went on that night, would go back and give great reports to their church. Very often I made it a point to thank that church several times from the stage on Sunday morning, announcing how many students received Christ and thanking its members for their participation in the event.

Events like this one demanded extra security. This gave me the opportunity to call up men I knew from area churches and ask them to be involved. Many of these men were so impressed with the event, they became financial supporters.

Every event or activity you plan involves planning, booking or recruiting. Document when you need to do this, transfer those tasks to whatever calendar you use, and even make some of the calls right then if necessary.

WHY PLAN AHEAD?

Regardless of whether we are full-time youth ministers or whether we are the pastor's sister who somehow got suckered into running junior high Sunday School, we have the opportunity to make an impact in the lives of young people. This privilege has been entrusted to us by God. We may be the only glimpse of God that a student sees. What does your program reflect? Excellence? Or whatever you can throw together because you are really busy?

Here's the ironic thing: If you plan the way I've discussed—taking the time to book things ahead of time, nailing down necessary details and planning ahead—you'll have *more time* and you'll open doors to opportunities for greater impact. Remember: "In reality, a well-administered ministry will provide more valuable time to spend with your students."[3]

WHAT DOES A YEAR SCHEDULE *LOOK* LIKE?

We talked about it; you've seen many of the details outlined; now let me show you what it looks like.

The following is a sample year schedule I planned out one summer. **Important Note:** This is a schedule for a campus outreach with the purpose of reaching unchurched kids with the gospel and plugging them in to the local church. My methods included a weekly Campus Life Club, volunteer staff members spending time with students weekly, activities and eventually a Bible study and taking students to church.

> **Note:** Most of the weekly agendas that I used for these Campus Life Live events (on the first Monday of the month) or Impact events (the other Mondays) are like the ones described in chapter 3. I have also put them on the website arranged by topic. Most of the events I've used are described in chapter 5 and on my website as well.

CAMPUS LIFE
1999/2000 CALENDAR

CENTER JUNIOR HIGH

Date	Event
Monday, September 13	First Campus Life Live
Monday, September 20	Free Root Beer Floats
Monday, September 27	Impact
Monday, October 4	Pizza Bash—All You Can Eat and Drink for $2
Monday, October 11	Impact-Friendship Club—Choices Wrap-Up
Friday, October 15	All Night Escape—Hoops, Hockey, Laser Tag, Pool, Nachos and Sodas All Night Long!!! Only $10
Monday, October 18	Impact
Monday, October 25	Impact
Monday, November 1	Campus Life Live Concert
November 5, 6, 7	Staff Retreat—Free, Fun and Fundamental for Our Staff Team!
Monday, November 8	Impact
Monday, November 15	Impact
Thursday, November 23	Thanksgiving
Monday, November 29	Impact
Friday Night, December 3	Winter Xtremz Citywide Junior High Event
Monday, December 6	Campus Life Live
Monday, December 13	Impact
CHRISTMAS VACATION	Staff One-on-One
Friday, December 24	Church Christmas Services
Monday, January 3	Campus Life Live—Earthball Blitz

January 14, 15, 16	Snow Retreat
Monday, January 10	Impact
Monday, January 17	Impact
Monday, January 24	Impact
Monday, January 31	Impact—Video Scavenger Hunt
Monday, February 7	Campus Life Live—"What's Up with Sex?"
Monday, February 14	Impact—Safe Sex
Monday, February 21	Impact
Monday, February 28	Impact
Friday, March 3	All Night Xtremz
Monday, March 6	Campus Life Live—Ray Johnston, "Why Church?"
Monday, March 13	Impact
Monday, March 20	Impact
Monday, March 27	Impact Team—Bigger and Better Hunt
April 3	Campus Life Live—Drugs and Alcohol Panel
Monday Night, April 10	Impact
April 15-20	Southern California Trip 2000
Monday Night, April 24	Impact
May 1	Last Campus Life Live
Monday Night, May 8	Impact
Monday Night, May 15	Impact Goes to Ice Cream
Monday Night, May 22	Last Impact

Notes

1. Jim Burns and Mike DeVries, *The Youth Builder* (Ventura, CA: Gospel Light, 2001), pp. 39-40.
2. Doug Fields, *Purpose-Driven Youth Ministry* (Grand Rapids, MI: Zondervan Publishing House, 1998), p. 63.
3. Burns and DeVries, *The Youth Builder*, pp. 39-40.

How Do I Recruit More Volunteers?

AN EFFECTIVE STRATEGY TO GET MORE HELP!

In July of 1998 I walked into the Youth for Christ office to find a file in my mailbox with a note from "the powers that be." Our ministry had lost a staff member, leaving a gap that needed to be filled.

Years before, a junior high campus had opened their doors to a campus outreach, an opportunity we couldn't pass up. In the absence of the former staff member, the ministry wanted me to pick it up and run with it.

So there I was with only a month and a half to build a staff, secure the facility and meet some kids. I looked through the file and the biggest hurdle was staring me in the face: only one existing staff member. I needed some volunteer staff immediately!

Ever needed volunteers? What do you do? Is it possible to build a staff quickly? The good news is that by September I started that outreach with eight weekly staff people and several other volunteers.

Keep this in mind: Building a staff might be hard for us, but it's very easy for God.

STEPS TO TAKE BEFORE YOU BUILD YOUR TEAM

There are those people who love to sit around and wait for someone to knock on the door. They may ask for prayer or even pray themselves, hoping to hear someone knock on the door. Very often no one knocks. We can pray for staff all we want, but sometimes God wants *us* to go get them.

> **Building a staff might be hard for us, but it's very easy for God.**

Did Noah *build* an ark, or did God drop it from the sky? Did the Israelites *collect* the manna or wait for it to be delivered to their door? Did Jesus walk around and *recruit* His disciples or wait for them to come knocking? What's the common denominator here? God is the One who provides, but we've got to use the knowledge, skills and abilities He's given us to do the work. He'll do His part, but we've got to do our part. Our part starts with two steps.

STEP ONE: REALIZE YOU CAN'T DO IT ALONE!

We can't do this work on our own. No matter how talented or gregarious you are, don't forget that God's the One who is going to build your staff. You're just the one lucky enough to be a part of what God is doing! In other words, without God, you've got no skills! Remember the words of Psalm 127:1: "Unless the LORD builds the house, its builders labor in vain." Don't get caught up in building the house on your own!

We can approach recruitment with one of two inappropriate attitudes: *I don't know anyone who will be on my staff team. There's no way I can do this!* or *I'm such a stud; I'm a staff-recruiting KING! I'll recruit this staff in no time.*

If you have either of those attitudes, go no further; you're dead in the water. God wants us to depend on Him for everything, even recruiting staff. I'm not overspiritualizing this; I'm telling the truth. Don't try it and then ask for God's blessing. Bring Him in at the beginning of the process. Pray specifically for God to help you, which leads you to step two.

STEP TWO: REMIND GOD WHAT HE PROMISED!

When I needed volunteers desperately, I reminded God what Jesus said in Matthew 9:37-38: "The harvest is plentiful but the workers are few. Ask the Lord of the harvest, therefore, to send out workers into his harvest field." Jesus tells us to ask God to send us workers. We need to depend on Him to make this process happen. Prayer reminds us that He is in charge and that He has promised to meet our needs in this area. Now we don't have to worry!

Ray Johnston of Bayside Church in the Sacramento, California, area always tells a story from when he was doing ministry in Marin County. He was overwhelmed with tons of kids and no staff. So one evening while driving home he pulled his car to the side of the road and read that verse in Matthew. Ray asked God with sincerity, "If You really can do it, I really need the help!" That week Ray started talking to people about the idea of helping out, and people were actually responding. He even had some people walk into his office and ask him if he needed any help. Ray says that he immediately drove to that exact same spot, got on his knees and asked God for a Porsche. No luck yet!

I tried what Ray said. I prayed and reminded God of that verse. I say "reminded God," but really I was reminding myself that God can do it. Guess what? God kept His end of the bargain.

BUILDING A STAFF TEAM

Okay, so you're ready to build a team, but you don't know where to start. Alrighty then, here we go!

BRAINSTORM

Write down the name of everyone you know who has the following qualifications:

1. They have a pulse.
2. They think God is number one in their life.

Remember, brainstorming isn't the time to decide whether or not you think they can do it. Brainstorming is simply writing down ideas. You'll edit the list later.

I can't tell you how many times in my years at Youth For Christ in Sacramento I almost edited somebody off the list before they were even on the list! In my mind I thought, *Oh, they'll never want to do this*, or *I haven't talked to them in years*. Each year my staff contains at least two or three people who I would never have guessed would help.

INVITE

Invite people you have listed to help you in your ministry *once* in a small way. It's that simple. Don't try to recruit them to join the staff for the rest of their lives. Don't give them a theology exam. Just tell them you really need help scooping ice cream this Wednesday. You want them to see what God's doing in the ministry so that they can become excited about it.

I have a friend named Jenny. Years ago I talked to Jenny about helping out weekly on my staff. Jenny seemed afraid of the commitment; after all, she was very busy. About a year later I was having a big pizza event that demanded the need for extra help. One of my staff recruited a bunch of people from his singles' class at church to help us out for the evening. Jenny, who was in that class, showed up to help. All night she was excited by what she saw. She came up to me afterwards and said, "We need to talk." Two weeks later she was helping us out weekly.

In sales there is a principle called "get the appointment." Don't try to sell them the product on the phone, but put it in front of them so you can show them the benefits—so that they can try it out and see themselves using it. The same goes for recruiting staff. So many of us call up our prospects and start laying out the commitment it takes and the time it requires. When we do that, we scare off the Jennys in our lives. Just "get the appointment." Invite them to help you out one time—no strings attached. Invite them to help with a legitimate need like scooping ice cream, serving pizza, driving a van, acting as weekend nurse or something else that allows them to get a taste of the ministry.

When you get people involved in ministry in small ways, the workers you want will float to the top. They'll fall in love with the students and ask *you* if they can help.

EVALUATE

I have made the mistake of skipping this step several times—a few of which have ended in catastrophe. Before asking someone if they want to help regularly, you *must* evaluate whether or not they are ready to be used by God. Remember, your requirements so far have been pretty slim. Now you need to find out if this old friend of yours is in the middle of an ugly divorce, has started drinking heavily or enjoys smashing headlights with a crowbar! You need to screen this person.

I like taking people to lunch and shooting the breeze, asking about their relationship with God and how they think God can use them. Through such interviews, you'll often be able to see what kind of character they have. Read 1 Timothy 3 for yourself; it gives a great outline of leadership qualities to look for.

Also, find out their heart, their passion. Don't overlook a hidden talent or resource that's sitting right next to you. The person you're recruiting may be the best up-front personality you've ever met or the answer to all your sound-system problems.

Make sure you evaluate your prospects. See if these are the people you want impacting your students' lives. Find out their abilities and skills, and help them find a place where they can use their gifts to serve God and further your ministry.

INVITE BACK

Invite prospective ministry helpers back again, and this time plant the question in their mind, *Does God want to use me in this ministry?* Don't ask for a commitment right then; just get them to come visit again with the understanding that you want to talk to them afterwards and see what God laid on their heart to do.

That's it. The Lord of the harvest has big things planned for your ministry. Trust in Him and be diligent with the abilities and knowledge He's given you.

Do Numbers Really Matter?

HOW CAN I MAKE OUR NUMBERS GROW?

One of the most frequent questions I receive via e-mail is "How can my youth group grow and reach more people?"

When I interviewed Jim Burns, he stated that the average youth-group size in America is 12, and it's run by a volunteer. Many youth leaders get discouraged with small numbers. Are small numbers bad? Many people say no! On the other hand, are we to look at small youth-group sizes that aren't growing in number and simply shrug our shoulders? Should we justify it by saying "That's OK. We're growing spiritually, so numbers don't matter"?

ABOUT THE NUMBERS

Very often, growth in numbers is a good measuring stick of God doing something exciting. Let's take a look at the Early Church:

- Praising God and enjoying the favor of all the people. And the Lord added to their number daily those who were being saved (Acts 2:47).
- But many who heard the message believed, and the number of men grew to about five thousand (Acts 4:4).
- Nevertheless, more and more men and women believed in the Lord and were added to their number (Acts 5:14).
- So the word of God spread. The number of disciples in Jerusalem increased rapidly, and a large number of priests became obedient to the faith (Acts 6:7).

I love to train staff and student leaders. I've trained 1,200 in a room, and I've trained 4! Even in the smallest town with the humblest youth groups, I've seen growth in numbers when God is doing something. It's a four-step process that works like this:

1. Kids grow in their faith.
2. Their faith becomes contagious, and they bring friends.
3. Friends are reached with the gospel, and they begin to grow.
4. Their faith becomes contagious, and they bring friends.

The process multiplies; do the math.

I just trained a group in a small town; you know the kind—if you blink while driving through, you'll miss it completely. Well, this town had a small country church that started with about 40 people. God has been using the pastor to reach the community and exciting things are happening. He preaches at two services in his little church with about 200 people coming each week. That's incredible growth for that town!

A small town like this usually only has a few students in the youth group. This pastor brought me in for a two-hour evangelism class for his student leaders. Eighteen students showed up! I've trained at churches 10 times that size and had fewer student leaders. How do some churches grow like that?

OK! Cut to the chase, Jonathan! How can our numbers increase?

PRAY!

Start by praying—and pray hard. Ask God to increase your group size. Sure, we all say we pray, but do we *really* pray? Take time out of each day to pray specifically for individual students and the friends they'll reach. Pray for God's direction in your programming and teaching. Pray for the students who drive you nuts. Pray that God will lay compassion on your heart—a compassion for lost students who you wouldn't normally reach out to. Be ready though—God will answer those prayers!

KEEP THE ONES YOU'VE GOT!

Give the students you already have something to bring their friends to. This means coming up with creative programming that students enjoy. Meet the needs of the students attending.

A lot of people take this one for granted. Why? Because it takes a lot of work: more work to arrange a bunch of vehicles for a video scavenger hunt; more work to find a video clip and set up all the media stuff to kick off a video discussion; more work to arrange an all-nighter with laser tag, skating, a gym, etc.; more work to prepare dynamic talks or put together a budget that brings in dynamic speakers. It's a lot more work—but it's *worth* it!

That's why I've dedicated my website to providing cutting-edge games, video clips, activities, discussions and programming ideas for free. Can't beat that with a stick!

> **Give the students... something to bring their friends to.**

We need to get students excited about what's going on so that they bring their friends to check it out.

So what should be going on? Make sure your ministry includes the following basic essentials:

- An event or program with a comfortable format for students to bring friends to. This may be a weekly program or just a once-a-month outreach. This could also be certain set events. The bottom line is that the unchurched need to feel like they belong!
- An opportunity to worship
- Scripture study
- Fellowship and fun—don't neglect this! Students are going to have it one way or another, and it may be up to you who they have it with.

Contacting Students Who Need Christ

Huh? This means meeting kids where they are and getting to know them: discovering their physical, emotional, social and spiritual needs. Guess what? Your students aren't the only ones who should be bringing students to youth group. You can meet students where they are and build relationships with them. This doesn't mean you walk up to a kid for the first time with a flyer in your hand; this means hanging out with students because you love them. If you like basketball, find where students play basketball and play with them. If you know students like to skateboard, provide a place for them to skateboard. If your ministry reaches a certain campus, go to those games and events to meet students.

Your students aren't the only ones who should be bringing students to youth group.

Once you contact students and get to know them, then you'll find opportunities to invite them to youth group or church. Here are a few ideas of where to contact kids:

- On campus during lunch
- School sports games
- The local teen hangout
- The fast-food place across the street from the school

Contacting doesn't stop outside of youth group. When students come to your weekly program, studies or events, use this as an opportunity to get to know them better. Here are some simple suggestions:

- Play on their teams during games.
- Shoot hoops, play Ping-Pong, or do whatever you have available in your church facility.
- Learn their names, notice their interests and ask them about their week.

BUILD RELATIONSHIPS WITH THEM

Once you get to know students better, you can begin to build relationships with them. You do this by hanging out with them and meeting their physical, emotional, social and spiritual needs.

Building relationships with students is one of the best ways you and your staff can spend time. Our weekly staff meeting always includes the staff member's report about their time with students that week. As we build relationships with students, we find opportunities to share the gospel, disciple them and equip them to reach out. Here are some great relationship building activities:

- Have them over to your home for movies, spa, games, etc.
- Take them shopping—Christmas gift shopping is a great opportunity!
- Use small groups as part of your program to get to know students better and open doors to deeper conversation. (Read more about this in chapter 9.)
- Take them to a Kings basketball game. (I'm from Sacramento, so give me a break!)
- Play laser tag.
- Go to miniature golf and video game places.
- Go to their house; meet their parents and siblings.

CREATE A MOMENTUM OF GROWTH

Notice the wording: "Create a momentum of growth." Many of us don't even talk about this; instead we talk about advertising. We make the mistake of thinking that advertising is simply handing out flyers or putting up posters. The truth is that cool flyers, posters and a big draw (e.g., food, activities, etc.) do not guarantee a good event. I saw a local church publish professional fliers and posters for an event that featured Ken Davis as the speaker. Ken Davis is incredible—and not the cheapest speaker either. The church targeted all the churches in the city, hoping to bring thousands out. About 70 people showed up.

This kind of advertising alone is futile. We need to plan our year strategically with programs or events that provide opportunities for the group to build up to a great event.

For example, if you're going to do a big pizza event to bring out a bunch of kids to your Tuesday night program, don't start the year off with *that* event. Some of us start the year out cold turkey with one big event, putting everything we've got into that event like a baby rattlesnake injecting all its venom in one bite.

Build momentum, starting the year off by bringing out as many students as you can—maybe that's only eight students. Encourage them to start bringing their friends. Build up the group's size using events like Manhunt (see p. 116), and let them know the pizza bash is coming. Finally, use the students—your most effective marketing tool—to bring back as many of their friends for that event as they can. You can always offer incentives such as a prize for the person who brings the most friends.

Once the momentum is built, feel free to advertise. Decide where the best place to do this is. If your purpose is to reach unchurched kids for Christ, then you don't want simply to announce it at youth group. You need to find a way to advertise on campus or at places where teens hang out. Effectively communicate the draw (e.g., free pizza). Posters and flyers can work more effectively now that you've established momentum.

DOES THIS REALLY WORK?

In 1993 I started a junior high campus outreach with the following resources at my fingertips: no students, no staff, no facility and a lot of prayer.

God provided one kid—a girl named Tonya, who had visited her cousin's youth group where my friend happened to be speaking. I called her up and told her about the fun stuff we were going to be doing. I said things like "Do you like the snow? We go on a snow trip every year. Do you like to water ski? We go on a water-ski trip every year. Do you like pizza? We're going to have a pizza feed for your school, all-you-can-eat pizza for a buck."

She was interested right away and brought her brother and five friends to meet me in a pizza place, my treat! I asked all her friends the same questions, finding out what they like to do for fun. At the end of the meal, I handed them a flyer with a map to my house. I told them next week was our first meeting, with free root beer floats.

The next week 12 kids came to my house. The original 7, minus 1 plus 6 new friends who came for root beer floats. When they all got there, I told them, "We're going to have root beer floats, but first, everyone get in a line!" Then we started the game where you reach your hand in a bucket and try to pull out a bar of soap (see p. 32). Soapy water splashed everywhere; the students laughed and had a great time. We played three or four games and then broke out the root beer floats before they had a chance to complain. During root beer floats we again talked about all the activities we were going to be doing that year, including a pizza bash in a few weeks. I told them that the next week we were going to have a great time as always and encouraged them to bring friends.

The next week we had 22 kids. The games got crazy, lamps got knocked over and my wife got nervous. Needless to say, the next week we were in the garage—with 35 students. It was then that I announced the pizza bash was in only two weeks. The next week we had a few more. I announced that they should bring friends, and the person who brought the most friends would get a prize.

We had 45 students in my garage for the pizza bash. By this time I had several staff members—people from my church who had heard about the exciting ministry in the garage.

Ministry continued in the garage for years. I tried talking to the school about running the program there—through Campus Life, who are on numerous campuses across the United States—but they always had an excuse for why we couldn't. A few years later a new principal was hired about the same time that some violence broke out on campus. We had a positive reputation in the community, so the school board approached us about helping out with the situation. I told them that I could help if I had access to the campus.

Within a year we were in the cafeteria on Wednesday nights with 200 students showing up. We came on campus at lunch, visited with kids, played ball, etc. God opened the doors and the ministry took off.

Yes, this really works. Your group has the potential to grow and reach your community for Christ. If you're ready to let God have the reins, He will do incredible things in your ministry.

Are Small Groups Worth It?

A CLOSER LOOK AT WHAT SMALL GROUPS CAN DO

Let's cut to the chase. Do you want a ministry tool that can provide the following benefits?

- A great way for students to get to know each other better
- A way for staff to build strong relationships with students
- A stepping-stone to accountability and mentor relationships
- An environment in which individuals can be heard
- An arena in which students can interact with and learn from others who might be going through similar struggles or situations

Interested? Well, maybe you don't have to read an entire book about small groups, but you want some quick tips. This chapter covers the basics.

SMALL-GROUP BASICS

START MEETINGS ON A LIGHT NOTE

It's that simple. In most small groups you don't want to sit down, look at the kid sitting across the circle and ask, "So what's the biggest sexual sin you committed this week?" In other words, don't start off with deep or vulnerable questions that could close doors before you even get to the front porch. Start with light questions that people want to answer.

In 9 out of 10 small groups, I start with the question, "What is your name and favorite kind of pizza?" I've never met a kid who didn't want to answer that unintimidating question. The idea is to bring up something that is fun to share. A few examples:

- What is your name and favorite kind of pizza?
- Share your name and the pet you would have if you could have any animal tamed in the world.
- Tell us your name and your favorite thing to do on a Friday night.
- Share your name and what you want for your next birthday.
- What is your name, and what kind of car would you want if I had millions of dollars and would buy it for you.

As you can see, the first part of starting light is asking that first fun question. Now most of us usually have a topic that we need to discuss, so we need to segue into that conversation. I usually do that by asking another fun, nonembarrassing question that delves into the topic, not getting too deep, but still getting on track with the meat of the discussion.

At this point, students will have answered two easy questions and have some positive momentum toward sharing answers. People like to be heard, and if the small group does its job, the members feel comfortable and safe to proceed into deeper conversation. I slowly go deeper with the questions as students feel more comfortable about opening up. The questions get deeper, maybe even more personal and more focused toward the heart of the topic.

Let's look at an example of the order in which I would ask questions in a small group where the topic is friendship.

1. Share your name and favorite kind of pizza.
2. Describe a good memory you have with a friend.
3. What qualities do you look for in a friend?
4. What qualities do you avoid in a friend?
5. Which of these qualities is something you might need to work on?

In this example you can see how the depth of the questions progresses toward number 5. You can also see that if you started off a small group with something like "All right, share your name and what friendship qualities you need to work on!" you could have trouble getting people to open up.

Start light, making it easy and comfortable for students to share; then slowly get deeper, creating a safe atmosphere where students want to open up and share their heart.

Start light, making it easy and comfortable for students to share; then slowly get deeper, creating a safe atmosphere where students want to open up and share their heart.

HAVE CLEARLY DEFINED BOUNDARIES, RULES AND EXPECTATIONS

Another good principle in running a small group is laying out boundaries, rules and expectations at the beginning. This doesn't mean you need to lay out the Ten Commandments the first time you meet; just voice your expectations and the direction for the group. Many students have no clue what a small group is, so don't assume they know. I've taken unchurched students to church services and youth-group meetings for years. I loved watching how they reacted to many of the *churchy* phrases that we use and think they understand. I'll never forget the time that I brought a group of students to a youth-group meeting and near the end of the evening the person up front declared, "Now it's time to form our small groups." A couple of the kids I brought looked at me with fear and asked, "What are small groups?"

I told them that each week they just divided into groups of about 8 to 10. They looked at me skeptically. "What do they do?" they asked.

Don't assume that students know what you're doing. Tell them what you hope to accomplish by meeting together in a smaller group. Communicate your expectations for attendance, for participation—even touch on conduct. I'll talk more about this in the tips section later in this chapter.

AIM FOR A CLEAR PURPOSE

Another one of the basics is knowing your purpose for having small groups. Frequently I ask youth workers what their purpose is for small groups. Many of them have trouble explaining exactly what their purpose is. Why? *They don't know!*

Clarify your purpose for having small groups. Do you simply want to provide an arena in which students can learn the material in a way other than from up-front talks? If that's the case, then your purpose would be to understand the material and your focus would be the topic. If your purpose is to deepen the relationships in the group, you might have a topic, but the purpose would be to provide a discussion that motivates students to open up and share their hearts with each other, increasing their level of trust and vulnerability with their small-group members and leader.

LISTEN!

It's simple. It's basic. It's often neglected, but it's one of the most important reasons for having a small group—giving students an opportunity to open up and feel heard. Notice I didn't say "be" heard; I said "feel" heard. Steven Covey calls this type of listening "empathetic listening" in his book *Seven Habits of Highly Effective People.* Covey argues that this kind of listening is more than just active listening, repeating back what you heard and communicating positive nonverbal signals.[1]

Empathetic listening seeks to understand the feelings and emotions behind the person. This is so very necessary in our work with kids. The walls that they put up are often thick and hard to break down. A staff person who doesn't listen empathetically can easily miss what's really going on inside a kid's head.

GROUP SIZE DETERMINES OUTCOME

The last small-group basic is not only an observation; it's a fact. As group size grows, impact shrinks. Now, before you get your feathers all ruffled, think about it. The more people you have in a group, the less each individual has an opportunity to be heard. As the group size gets bigger, trust gets smaller and people open up less. The less people open up, the less they grow.

FIVE TIPS TO GUARANTEE *INEFFECTIVE* SMALL GROUPS

That's right, if you're going to mess up, mess up *big time*! Follow these tips and your small groups will suffer immensely. Here are the ludicrous tips, followed by explanations of what you should *really* be doing.

DON'T HAVE ANY SMALL-GROUP RULES!

Let everyone talk at once, thrash on each other and disrespect the leader.

Seriously, folks! Introduce the small group as a time to express ourselves and hear from each other. But to do that we need two rules: be honest and respect others. I always tell the group that I'm looking forward to hearing from them—then I get specific. I'll say something like, "When Jenny is talking, we all listen. Then when we talk, Jenny's going to listen to us."

Part of respecting other members of the group means being confidential with what's shared in the group. Don't be afraid to express this. Let people know that what they share is safe in the group and won't be joked about with others later.

The younger the group, the more you have to establish the rules. Regardless, it's good to remind people about respecting each other. You can get as detailed as the group needs you to be.

Don't Give Everyone an Opportunity to Answer Each Question!

As soon as a couple of people speak out, move on to the next question.

Really now! Give everyone in the group an opportunity to respond to each question. After you ask a question, go around the circle and ask each person what they think. Some small-group leaders like to affirm that it's okay to pass or abstain from answering. I choose not to offer passing as an option. I find that if students know they can simply pass, it's an easy way out of having to open up. If the subject matter is deep, I make it a point to read nonverbal signals and make sure students aren't put on the spot.

Talk a Lot!

Always finish sentences for kids, and give long examples from your own life that illustrate your point.

Come on! You've got two ears and one mouth; use them proportionally. This isn't our chance that we've been waiting for to preach to a captive audience (or an audience held captive, in most cases). If your group is having trouble sharing or talking, don't blabber on. Ask the question in a different way. Give examples of possible answers. Sometimes it helps if you answer first; but answer as a member of the group—don't start preaching. Remember, this is their opportunity to feel free to open up and feel heard!

Race Through the Questions as Fast as Possible

See how fast you can finish your small group in order to get to the free time!

It's not a bad thing to allow someone to expand on a question. Question some of their answers further; there is no need to rush through them. The small-group leader sets the pace for the group. If the leader promotes quick answers, that's what the group will give. You don't need to draw things out and run them into the ground—that would be ludicrous tip number four—but don't miss an opportunity for someone to open up because they feel like they need to hurry. This isn't a race to see whose small group finishes first. Make sure you give everyone a chance to answer and to share their feelings on the subject. You may need to structure the meeting's time schedule so that there isn't pressure to finish within an inadequate amount of time, and yet allow for groups that do finish early to move into another activity rather than sit around trying to make small talk. Or give small-group leaders some additional ideas or questions to use in the event their group is not as talkative.

DON'T PREPARE A WRAP-UP

Just share what pops into your head. God will give you what you need to say.

Oh, puh-leeze! Prepare your wrap-up as best as you can beforehand. The wrap-up may be done when you pull the whole group together—if that's your format. Small groups are designed to raise questions and provide some direction for answers and conclusions. Don't let an unclear wrap-up create any more confusion. The wrap-up should always point to the answer that God gives, as well as some direction to find out more about it. Being prepared doesn't hinder the Spirit's leading; in actuality it gives you time to listen for the leading of the Holy Spirit so that you can be prepared for whatever occurs during the meeting!

A DEEPER LOOK AT SMALL GROUPS

We've gone over small-group basics and some quick tips. But let's step back and look a little deeper at this thing we call a small group. Small groups are a very effective tool that many youth workers use to provide some of the above results. But what is a small group, really?

The label "small group" is used loosely by youth workers. I've seen a lot of different creations labeled "small groups." Some are very organized and defined, so much so that if someone else runs a small group differently, they are looked down upon. Many youth workers simply use small groups as a part of their program. There may be a time for having the whole group together and then a time when the group is divided into smaller groups—hence the name "small groups." Others might refer to their Bible studies or care groups as small groups. Then there are those who create an actual ministry model called small groups which isn't merely a part of a program—it *is* the program and has a specific purpose.

Doug Fields touches on this subject in his book *Purpose-Driven Youth Ministry*. If I may insert a parenthetical here (Wow, did you see that? I started a parenthetical without using parentheses! Is that legal? If you haven't read his book, GO BUY IT! It's available at most Christian bookstores, and it has plenty of good ideas, examples and, most importantly, principles that guide you as you cast vision for your youth ministry.) Such is my parenthetical. Now back to small groups. Doug argues that a group of 15 is not a small group. Now, I've heard many youth workers claim that their youth group is a small group, which is understandable since the average youth group in America has 12 regularly attending students. Doug contends that 15 students is actually a crowd and that a group of four or five kids is optimum for true small groups.[2]

That's fine and dandy for groups with a good staff-to-student ratio, but youth worker after youth worker has asked me, "What if I have 30 kids, 3 staff, *including me and my wife*, and I need to divide into small groups? Should I just tell 15 kids to leave?"

Good question—and I'm not going to answer it! Answering that question is working backwards. Let's see what type of small group we want; then let's figure out what is possible with the resources and staff we have (or need to develop).

THREE TYPES OF SMALL GROUPS

Doug adequately defends his statement with a description of three types of small groups. These descriptions are worth looking at, because each level has a different degree of impact.

Level 1 Small Group

This is the type of group that is simply a part of the program. A large-group program meets together and, at a specific time, breaks up into small groups. People are randomly placed in these groups, so there is no consistency from meeting to meeting and no accountability is established. Doug contends that the impact of these groups is low. It's simply a means to an end, a necessary part of a program, not a catalyst for students to build deeper relationships with each other.

Level 2 Small Group

This type of group also meets as a part of the program. These groups, however, have the same students each week, thus having a medium level of consistency. Students have a chance to interact with the same students each week. The purpose is to get through a given set of questions or to discuss a certain topic. The level of impact is much higher. Relationships can deepen, and depending on the small-group leader, some accountability can be encouraged.

Level 3 Small Group

This type of small group focuses more on the students than the teaching. Content may be a starting place for discussion, but the focus is on building relationships and accountability. Here the small group *is* the program. The goal isn't to get bigger, but to grow deeper.

HANDLING GROWTH IN NUMBERS

So back to the question about how to handle large numbers. First, you need to ask yourself what kind of group you want to run. If you're running a Level 1 Small Group, I don't think the difference between a group of 5 and 10 is going to have a drastic effect. However, as you increase the level of accountability and focus on relationship building, each individual over five or six students may take away from the group as a whole.

So does this mean that we shouldn't try to attract new students to youth group? That sounds like an apostle-Paul question, so let me give you an apostle-Paul answer: May it never be! Don't ever stop reaching out to new students. I must admit, however, Doug's Level 3 Small Group produces a rather large hurdle; the youth worker needs to be proactive about consistently recruiting and developing new small-group leaders to form new groups with new students.

Bo Boshers, director of student ministries at Willow Creek Community Church in Chicago, has an interesting approach to this dilemma that he outlines in his book *Student Ministry for the Twenty-First Century*. Bo suggests that every small group is made up of a leader and an apprentice leader. This apprentice leader gets on-the-job training as the group grows and develops. Then, as the group gets too big, the group can split and the apprentice leader can lead their own group.[3]

I've heard a number of people voice worries about splitting a group. It can be hard. But I look at it like a church plant. The church owns from the beginning that it wants to grow (in depth) and expand (in numbers). If this is owned from the beginning, the group is ready—not always excited, but ready—for this.

Make Reaching a Priority

Since Bo's plan builds apprentice leaders into the small groups, this allows him to make it a goal to expand the group's size, hoping the group will grow big enough to launch a new small group.

How can we make our groups expand in number? Bo uses a tool called the "empty seat." The small-group leader teaches the value of evangelism from the first day of the group. The group owns the idea of bringing new friends into the group or seeking out individuals for the group. Weekly, the group shares the names of people who could fill the empty seat and prays for them specifically. This empty-seat philosophy is very much like the Billy Graham organization's Operation Andrew. People pray for three friends who they can bring to the Billy Graham Crusade. These types of tools are great because they teach individuals to pray for their lost friends and to seek out opportunities to invite their friends to a comfortable atmosphere in which they can hear the gospel and be involved hands-on with the evangelism process.

BOTTOM LINE

So what do I do now? Good question. Here are the steps.

DO SOME RESEARCH

If you're reading this book, you're already on your way. Don't stop here. Also check out what other youth leaders with small-group leadership experience think and what they've learned over the years. Check out more books like Doug's and Bo's.

RUB SHOULDERS

Find youth workers in your area that run small-group ministries. Take them out to lunch and pick their brains. Ask them questions about the issues discussed in this chapter. Visit their small groups and notice what works and what doesn't.

PRAY

Pray for God to give you guidance through this process. Seek out where He's leading you in your ministry. If you feel like He's speaking to you about evangelism lately, you may want to consider an idea like Bo's empty seat.

LET THE TEAM OWN THE DECISION

In his book *Twenty-One Irrefutable Laws of Leadership,* John Maxwell introduces the Law of Solid Ground. In this law of leadership, he contends that you don't make major decisions by yourself and then drop them like a bomb as a command for the leaders to follow.[4] Include leaders in this process. Have them own the decision with you so that they will be excited about it and carry it out with as much passion as you have.

REMEMBER THE BASICS

Many of the methods people use are simply their opinion, but don't forget the hard facts. Certain truths remain and must be considered when implementing your small-group program. Keep in mind that the larger the group, the less chance an individual has to develop trust in and open up to the group. Keep in mind that this is not an arena for leaders to preach. Know these truths, and let them guide you through this process.

Notes

1. Stephen R. Covey, *Seven Habits of Highly Effective People* (Thorndike, ME: G.K. Hall, 1997), n.p.
2. Doug Fields, *Purpose-Driven Youth Ministry* (Grand Rapids, MI: Zondervan Publishing House, 1998), pp. 143-144.
3. Bo Boshers, *Student Ministry for the Twenty-First Century* (Grand Rapids, MI: Zondervan Publishing House, 1997), n.p.
4. John C. Maxwell, *Twenty-One Irrefutable Laws of Leadership* (Nashville, TN: Thomas Nelson, 1998), n.p.

How Do I Plan Professional Programs?

CUTTING-EDGE PROGRAMS THAT DRAW STUDENTS IN

In chapter 9, the focus was on strategies to make your group grow and be more effective. Some important principles in building youth groups were outlined, including some good programming principles. That gave you a good look at how programming can be used for growth. Chapter 7 detailed planning ahead and getting specific programs on the calendar in accordance with your purpose. In this chapter, we will look specifically at how to plan a single program. What are the steps involved, from start to finish, in planning a professional program?

FIND A PURPOSE OR THEME

Finding a purpose or theme doesn't necessarily mean that you need a discussion topic theme (e.g., Knowing God). This might simply mean understanding your purpose (e.g., to reach unchurched kids for Christ or to bring out a large number of new kids to youth group and show them a good time). Just as we discussed in chapter 7, you should always know the purpose for meeting. The event purpose should be in line with your ministry's purpose statement. "Bringing new kids out" is in accordance with a purpose statement that includes outreach.

BRAINSTORM

Brainstorm for the best possible ideas to fulfill your purpose. If your purpose is to bring out a large number of new kids to youth group and show them a good time, you may come up with ideas like free pizza or giant sumo-wrestling pits. During the brainstorming process, no idea is bad. Dream about even the most crazy, impossible things.

INCORPORATE YOUR IDEAS WITH YOUR RESOURCES

Now it's time to get back to reality. If your brainstorm idea is to send every new kid to Hawaii for a vacation, here's where your budget tells you that this is impossible and that you'll just have to send them to Fresno (for us California folks). Incorporate these ideas with your budget, workers and supplies. For instance, let's say we came up with an outreach event that specifically has a purpose of bringing out a large number of new kids to youth group to show them a good time. In brainstorming, we come up with the idea of having free pizza, skateboard ramps, girls in bikinis, sumo wrestling and 12 kegs of beer (a liberal brainstorming team!).

Now that it's time to incorporate it with our resources. We realize that our church would never allow us to have girls in bikinis or beer as a draw (duh!), but we do need to evaluate some of the other stuff.

Budget

The first thing to evaluate is the budget. If we are hoping to draw 200 students to this event we are going to need a lot of pizza. I always plan one large pizza for every 3.5 students (a ratio that I came up with over the years). Two hundred students divided by 3.5 is 57 large pizzas. You have a contact with a pizza place that gives you large pepperoni pizzas for $7 each. So you'll need $400 for the pizza.

You realize from your past pizza events that you need drinks. You don't want to spend too much, so you take someone's suggestion to buy that red punch that comes in bulk at Costco. This should be another $30 you'll need to spend on punch, plus $15 on cups and plates. Your sumo-wrestling pit rental is $300, and let's say your local Youth For Christ has a guy who brings out skateboard ramps as a ministry. So far, so good. But your pastor says you really should give the skateboard guy's ministry at least $100 for his time. So that's another $100. You figure out that you're going to give away some prizes at the event and you're going to print up some really cool flyers. Luckily, you can do the flyers in-house! Lastly, always include a 10 percent cushion for incidental things that come up.

So your budget looks like this so far:

Pizza	$400
Drinks	$30
Paper products	$15
Sumo pit	$300
Skateboard/YFC	$100
Prizes	$50
10% cushion	$90
Subtotal	**$985**

After your spouse gets out the smelling salts and wakes you up, you look at your budget again and get really depressed. Why? Because you only have $42.78 in your youth ministry budget right now.

Now it's decision time. If you're sure you can bring out 200 students to this event, you charge kids each $5 and you'll end up $15 in the black.

It is important at this point to ask yourself if the money just interfered with your purpose. In this case, would charging $5 cause you not to bring as many students or the type of students that you want to bring? If the answer is yes, then your other option is fund-raising.

Many of you reading this will see visions of car washes when you read the word "fund-raising." That's not what I'm talking about. What I would do is approach some godly Christian people in my church and present them with what we're trying to do. I would then ask them if they would like to be one of 10 sponsors who would make this event happen. (If you're raising $1,000 and you asked someone to be one of 10 sponsors, you just asked them for $100.) This kind of fund-raising may be foreign to some of you. But it is a great way to do what is discussed in chapter 2 concerning bringing people alongside your ministry team. When the event comes around, you can invite these people to see the students who were drawn in because of their sponsorship.

I've heard many people—both in small churches and in big ones—say "We just can't afford to do large-scale events like that." I say you can't afford *not* to. Don't let the numbers scare you. You'll never *do* big if you can't *think* big.

Always remember, budget is an important part of your resources. As great as your brainstorming might be, you can only do what you can finance.

Workers

The second part of incorporating your ideas with your resources is to evaluate how many people you need to pull this event off. How much security? If you have people skateboarding, I would definitely have medical personnel there, preferably an athletic trainer or someone who's used to wrapping ankles or fixing head cuts. Do you need workers to serve the pizza? What about running the wrestling pit?

Write down a list of workers you have and figure out how much extra help you need. Recruiting extra help, as discussed in chapter 5, is a great way to expose potential volunteers to your ministry. Take advantage of this opportunity and get some potential staff members there to help out!

Supplies

The other resource you need to consider is your own supplies. Do you have coolers for the punch, tables for the pizza, caution tape for the border of the skateboard area and ropes and stands to rope off places for people to stand in line?

Make a list of all the supplies you need. If you don't already have them, you'll need to add those costs to your budget.

ADVERTISE!

Now it's time to market the event. You'll need to decide the best places to do this. If your purpose is to reach unchurched kids for Christ, then you don't want to just announce it at youth group. You need to find a way to advertise on campus and in places where teens hang out in your area. Also, you need to communicate effectively what the draw is (e.g., free pizza).

I've seen tons of events fail, not because they were bad ideas, but because they were poorly marketed or advertised. Too many people have learned the hard way that cool flyers and posters and a big draw do not guarantee a good event. I saw a local guy plan a cool outreach event with free pizza at a pool hall. He made great flyers and even had access to campus to hand them out. Pizza, pool, flyers—how could he go wrong? Only four people showed up. He lost hundreds of dollars and ate pizza for a month!

In chapter 9, I introduced an important concept in advertising: momentum. If you're going to do a big pizza event to bring out a bunch of kids to your Tuesday night program, don't start the year off with that event. Build momentum. Start the year off by bringing out as many students as you can, and then have them start bringing their friends. Build up the group's size using events like Manhunt (p. 116) and let them know the pizza bash is coming.

Finally, use students—your most effective marketing tool—to bring their friends to the event. You can always offer incentives, like prizes for the person who brings the most friends.

MOTIVATE ATTENDANCE

I've always used a student leadership team to help me with the planning process. This develops student leaders in my group and helps me pull off better events. As we just mentioned, students are our most effective marketing tool. All the work that goes into a program is futile if your leaders don't show up. It's hard to build momentum when your leaders can't even come! From day one drill your leaders

> **Build into your leaders from day one the importance of attendance. A student leader who can't attend isn't a student leader.**

on the importance of attendance. A student leader who can't attend isn't a student leader.

But you should involve more students than just the student leaders in this. All students can be motivated to attend and to bring their friends. Use as many students as possible to help make sure your attendance goals are met.

HOW TO RUN A PROGRAM

A program is the part of an event where students gather together to participate in or simply watch a message being communicated from a stage. Usually if the students have already been drawn there, the program has simply to keep their interest enough to communicate the intended message.

How do you plan a program, especially with big audiences? Are there rules to running something like this on stage? Youth For Christ in Sacramento has a big junior high event a couple times a year called XtremZ. We have a lot of fun and share the gospel—and every year kids come to Christ! In December of 2000 we had one of these events, and my job was to run the program. This event brings out over 1,000 people.

So what do you do with an audience of over 1,000 students? Good question. It's not like you can roll up a newspaper and start playing Newspaper Name Smack (see p. 38)! Well, again consider the purpose of the event. XtremeZ's purpose was to provide an event to which churches could bring junior high outreach students. Some ministries were outreaches. Others were church groups who tried to bring a lot of unchurched junior high kids. At the event we showed them a good time, shared the gospel and gave an invitation for kids to accept Christ.

So what do you do for the program portion of the event you are planning? Many people go straight to up-front games, which often work. But what about games that involve the whole audience? What do you do that entertains, yet doesn't take away from the speaker?

THE CHALLENGE

1. The audience should be happy to be there right away! In the first 30 seconds after junior high students sit down for a program they are asking

themselves, *Is this going to stink or what?* Answer that question with a big fat NO right away! Get them involved. Don't let them sit there on their bums and get bored!

2. Get the audience used to looking and listening to what is up front (as opposed to talking with their friends next to them, as if they're in a coffee bar with stage entertainment as background music).

3. Create a smooth segue from your activities to your speaker! Don't give them a reason to tune out because "the fun's over and the speaker has begun."

So how did we pull it off at our event? By God's grace! Psalm 127:1 says that "unless the LORD builds the house, its builders labor in vain." Don't leave God out of the process. I've messed up plenty of events that God blessed regardless! Here is what we did with God behind the wheel.

The Preshow

We had a preshow emcee entertain the students from the time they sat down until the show started. The emcee brought up two kids, one on each side of the stage; then he had four friends of each kid duct tape him to the wall. Each half of the crowd cheered for the team on their side of the room. In the meantime, the emcee encouraged everyone to be seated and let them know when the program would be starting.

The Countdown

Our preshow emcee counted down from 10 to the awaited start time, and an offstage microphone introduced the two emcees for the evening.

The All-Play Game

In order to get the entire crowd involved right away, we played a crowd game called the Saran Wrap Body Pass. We immediately got four staff members from the crowd (remembering Jonathan's Seven Deadly Sins tips, we had these people prearranged and ready) and had each of them stand in front of a given section of crowd that cheered for their staff member. Each staff member grabbed about three or four kids to wrap them (again, prearranged). Handing each group three or four rolls of plastic wrap, we told them to wrap the staff members as mummies when I yelled "Go!" (I always tell the staff to put their hands in the air so they have them free for later. Also, it's a really good idea to make sure the face is off-limits; plastic wrap isn't exactly breathable!)

When they were wrapped up, I asked the crowd what they thought the best way to judge who is wrapped the best might be; then I announced that I had an idea. "Pick them up and pass them to the back of the crowd and back up front again. First section to do that wins!" (Helmets aren't a bad idea!)

The Up-Front Game

After the all-play game, we usually play one up-front game so that the students are entertained and their focus is directed to the stage. For example, we would draw five names from the audience (from the cards they filled out as they arrived) and bring them onstage; each one would win a prize. My assistant walked onstage with a big box labeled "Box 1" and we began to play Let's Make a Deal (see p. 34).

The Transition

Program transitions are essential for junior high audiences because if you have even a five-second dull moment, everyone in your audience turns to the person next to them and starts discussing plans for later.

At this XtremZ event my co-emcee, who has a good command of an audience, used the last prize we awarded, a certificate to the next event, to talk about the speaker at that XtremZ and how much he meant to him. I interjected a word or two about that night's speaker, how much kids had enjoyed him in the past and how they requested to have him back. Then we prayed before we brought up the speaker. This got the audience quiet and focused.

The Speaker

I always use a funny speaker at this yearly event. Humor breaks down walls, crosses racial barriers and keeps students' attention. The speaker shared the gospel and a couple hundred kids came forward to receive Christ (67 made first-time decisions that night—praise God!).

The Final Fifteen

What then? We had about 200 kids leave the room with over 100 adult counselors. Now we had 15 minutes to kill before the end of the program.

We used this excellent opportunity for the speaker to talk to the remaining crowd and share some final words. Each speaker handles this differently.

The Final Game

Finally, we had some more fun! We played Ice Chest (see p. 23). A bunch of guys on stage getting ice poured down their T-shirts was a big hit!

HOW TO MESS UP A PROGRAM SO STUDENTS WON'T COME BACK

If you're going to mess up, mess up good. Do any of the following, and you'll have lame events that no students will ever attend.

Don't Be Prepared

If you really want to make sure students won't come back, just throw together your program that night at the last minute. Don't have any props ready for the games and make sure the crowd has to wait while you get your stuff in gear!

You can also guarantee failure by not screening your testimonies or talks. Have your average Joe stand up there, ready to wing it. They'll always say really interesting things that make everyone feel at ease! (Yeah, right!)

Only Include the In-Crowd

You can make people feel like they don't belong by using just the popular kids up front. Use them over and over again, and use private jokes that only they understand. Make sure they giggle up front and choose only their friends in all the games.

Use Weak Transitions

The best way to do rotten transitions is to just stand there when one thing is done and ask, "So what's next?" Then whip out a piece of paper and read what's next while the crowd sits and picks their noses!

Make Kids Feel Like They Don't Belong

That's right! Use alienating language and make condescending references to unbelievers. Make your program geared only toward the kid who has grown up in the church and understands Christianese!

This is especially true in an event that has the purpose of outreach. When you try to do an outreach event for unchurched kids, use words and phrases that only the church kids understand. Use the word "Christian" a lot and assume that everyone there knows what a Christian is. Talk about how bad non-Christians are and how sad it is that so many of them don't even come to church, know verses or (gasp!) even own a Bible. If you lead worship, start by saying "You'll all know this song," and then lead the singing without providing the words. After all, they should know the music—if they don't, then they're pagans and we really don't want that element around anyway!

Encourage Kids Only to Hang Out with Their Friends

This is a great principle for student leaders who don't want to reach others. I mean, let's face it, students have issues. We can't expect them to actually hang out with someone other than their friends. They shouldn't reach out to anyone outside their own little clique; Jesus probably wouldn't like those others anyway!

Don't Participate or Pay Attention to What's Going On

Sure, everyone is watching the staff and seeing how they act, but they really should mind their own business. Just don't wonder why no one is paying attention 'cuz they just followed your example!

Really folks, you are watched. I go to tons of events where the youth leaders all stand around the edge instead of mixing with the kids and sitting among them. Huge mistake! Use this opportunity to hang out with them as well as to be interested yourself. Who knows, God just might have something to say to *you* in the message!

What Are the Basics of Student Leadership?

BUILDING THE NEXT GENERATION OF YOUTH WORKERS

Student leadership should be one of the basics of youth ministry. Sadly, it is often one of the most neglected ministry models. It's usually filed on the bottom shelf as "something to do later when we have time." Then we never get to it because we've got to plan that next lesson, call back that disgruntled parent or vacuum the minivan we borrowed for the retreat. Besides, is student leadership really that important? Can't we just make sure that kids are growing in their faith?

Good questions. Luckily, we have a biblical example of a ministry worth copying—the ministry of Jesus. A close examination of Jesus' ministry reveals the importance of a student leadership program in our ministry. In this chapter, we'll examine Jesus' ministry and learn about the three types of students that make up the youth we're trying to reach. Then we'll lay out a tangible model of what a student leadership program like this can look like in our ministry.

THE JESUS MINISTRY MODEL

If we take a good look at Jesus' ministry, we'll see that it included service, outreach, teaching, growth and a student leadership program. Furthermore, I see Him reaching three different groups.

THE THOUSANDS

We all remember the stories of Jesus speaking to crowds of thousands. All through the Gospels huge crowds would gather around Him as He preached, taught and healed. Sometimes, weary of the crowds, He'd slip away to get some time of solitude, yet the crowds would still find Him. I can't help but respect Him for His attitude when this happened. He always welcomed them and ministered with compassion.

> But the crowds found out where he was going, and they followed him. And he welcomed them, teaching them about the Kingdom of God and curing those who were ill (Luke 9:11, *NLT*).

One of the by-products of healing and feeding people and of meeting their basic physical needs is *large crowds*! Jesus ministered to large crowds, both sinners and religious people, meeting their physical needs and then telling them the truth about what a relationship with God looks like. Jesus didn't have time to rub shoulders with everyone in the crowd. But those who were interested in following Him would show up again and again.

We can all reach students at this level. We reach crowds of students through ministry models that meet their physical, emotional and social needs, and then we tell them the truth about what a relationship with God is like. We might not have thousands, but we have a crowd. As leaders, we don't have time to rub shoulders with everyone in the group, but we can give them opportunities to get more deeply involved.

This group of kids can be labeled many things. I've heard them referred to as "curious kids" or "fringe kids." Regardless, this is the crowd of students that may be just checking things out. My prayer is that we, as youth workers, can look at these students through the same eyes through which Jesus looked—eyes of compassion.

He felt great pity for the crowds that came, because their problems were so great and they didn't know where to go for help. They were like sheep without a shepherd (Matthew 9:36, *NLT*).

Once I was meeting with a youth pastor who invited me to speak at his camp. He had hundreds of students in his ministry—quite a crowd. But he said something I'd like to hear more often. He said, "It would be easy to look at all these kids and think, *Great! My goal is accomplished. Hundreds of students. One of the largest in the area.* But who am I fooling? The campus across the street has 2,400 students. I don't even have 10 percent of them. My work's not close to being done."

This youth worker looked at crowds of kids, and his gut ached with compassion because they were lost like sheep without a shepherd. We need to be constantly reaching out to this group of students in our ministry.

THE HUNDREDS

You will also notice a tighter group that followed Jesus around. This was a group made up of many of His regular followers, including His twelve disciples, some people He had healed and some women.

Not long afterward Jesus began a tour of the nearby cities and villages to announce the Good News concerning the Kingdom of God. He took his twelve disciples with him, along with some women he had healed and from whom he had cast out evil spirits. Among them were Mary Magdalene, from whom he had cast out seven demons; Joanna, the wife of Chuza, Herod's business manager; Susanna; and many others who were contributing from their own resources to support Jesus and his disciples (Luke 8:1-3, *NLT*).

This group probably numbered 100 people or more. Jesus not only had the disciples and the regular followers, but He had the 72 other disciples that had spent time with Him and were advocates for His ministry.

The Lord now chose seventy-two other disciples and sent them on ahead in pairs to all the towns and villages he planned to visit (Luke 10:1, *NLT*).

Even after Jesus was killed, the remaining loyals of this group still gathered together.

During this time, on a day when about 120 believers were present, Peter stood up and addressed them (Acts 1:15, *NLT*).

This is the group from which they chose the new disciple—the replacement for Judas. Good thing Jesus was developing more than just the Twelve.

We know students in this category. Maybe there aren't a hundred of them, but these are students who are regular attendees and are ready to grow. Some people refer to these students as "casual kids" or "regulars." Regardless, these are the students who are beyond the stage of just checking things out. They actually have an interest in growing in their faith. It may be just a small desire to attend a Bible study or small group, or it could be a strong conviction to grow closer to God. Potential student leaders exist in this group.

THE TWELVE

We are all also aware that Jesus invested time and effort in the Twelve. He chose twelve disciples to train, teach, develop and take with Him to minister to others.

As a result, Jesus stopped his public ministry among the people and left Jerusalem. He went to a place near the wilderness, to the village of Ephraim, and stayed there with his disciples (John 11:54, *NLT*).

Jesus developed relationships with disciples as individuals, getting to know them personally. Sometimes He would even hang out with a small group of them.

About eight days later Jesus took Peter, James, and John to a mountain to pray (Luke 9:28, *NLT*).

We also have an opportunity to develop an intimate group of students in our ministries, students who aren't there just checking things out, students who don't merely want to grow, but who are ready to develop their spiritual gifts and be used by God to reach and serve others. These students are sometimes labeled "core kids," "student leaders" or "committed kids."

How can you take the step to create a group like this? Do you simply do like Jesus did and walk into McDonald's to two kids who are cooking the fries and say, "Come follow me?" I can see it now: "And they left their fry trays at once and followed him."

A STUDENT LEADERSHIP MODEL

Let's see what an effective student leadership team can look like.

SELECTING POSSIBLE STUDENT LEADERS

The first thing to think about is how you're going to select student leaders. You could simply select them; after all, that's what Jesus did. But that method proved to be inefficient because, hey, He got Judas. (I'M KIDDING!) Many youth workers prefer selecting students. That way they can choose students who've demonstrated a strong character and potential to serve God in this way. The drawback with this method is that we are not the Messiah (even though we all know a few workers who think they are), and we might miss some good prospects whom God can use. We need to admit our limitations.

People judge by outward appearance, but the LORD looks at a person's thoughts and intentions (1 Samuel 16:7, *NLT*).

Very often we may choose the charismatic leader of the youth group, who's coincidentally sleeping with his girlfriend, and miss the shy, backward student who is the next Dwight L. Moody (or the next Doug Fields, for you young'uns).

With this in mind, I like to open it up for students to apply. I announce it for several weeks and make applications available (see appendix B). I also like to request that students have to ask me or a staff member for an application. This simple request seems to filter out some of the students who aren't terribly motivated.

Another step that I take is requiring all student leaders to find a Christian mentor who they will meet with weekly. They actually have a form that they give to an adult mentor to fill out, which is due when they turn in their application.

The application for student leadership involves more than just a simple name and address form. This is an overview of the program stating the requirements and expectations of the leadership team along with a detailed application with several questions about the student's faith, personal walk and skills. On the next few pages are samples of what our My Commitment, Ministry Area Choices, and Will You Be My Mentor? sheets look like.

3. Why do you want to be on the Student Leadership Team?

Reproducibles | 227

4. How would your unchurched friends describe your relationship with God?

5. How would your churched friends describe your relationship with God?

6. How would your family describe your relationship with God?

226 | Appendix B

STUDENT LEADERSHIP APPLICATION

Basic Information   ❑ Male ❑ Female

Name _____

Address _____ E-mail _____

Phone(s) _____

Parent/Guardian's Name(s) _____

Grade_____ School _____

Just for Kicks

Favorite thing to do for fun _____

Favorite type of music _____

Favorite movie _____

Your Relationship with God

1. Please share when and how you became a Christian.

2. Please share what you are doing to continue to grow in your faith in Christ.

© 2002 Gospel Light. Permission to photocopy granted. The Top 12 Resources Youth Workers Want

Sample

MY COMMITMENT

I have a personal relationship with Jesus Christ and live by faith, following His example and His commands in the Bible.

I AM COMMITTED TO

- Regular church and youth-group attendance
- Modeling a healthy commitment to my family
- Personal growth through regular Bible study and prayer
- A weekly meeting with an adult mentor for Bible study, memorization and accountability
- A lifestyle befitting one who is a role model and an ambassador of Christ
- Being an example of proper behavior during worship services, programs and activities
- Being Christ's light on my campus, in my neighborhood and in my home

I AM EXCITED ABOUT

- Volunteering a minimum of two hours a week, in addition to regular youth programs and activities, in a specific ministry area (see Ministry Area Choices page 184)
- Attending bimonthly Impact meetings on the second and fourth Sundays of the month
- Attending the Impact Development Retreat on June 10-12
- Completing regular reading assignments

TRAINING AND DEVELOPMENT DETAILS

Bimonthly Leadership Meetings

- Prayer time

- Student-led Bible studies
- Discussion of assigned reading
- Ministry reports/decisions
- Training
- Working in ministry area teams

Leadership Retreat (June 14 and 15)

- Worship/Fellowship
- Christian Character
- Using Programs That Reach Different Students
- Brainstorming Multiplication/Outreach
- Discovering and Developing Your Spiritual Gifts

Ministry Areas

- Thursday night leadership team
- Outreach team
- Contact team
- Special events team
- Drama team
- Junior high staff team
- Admin team

Training Topics

- Leading a Bible Study
- Planting a Seed/Sharing Your Faith
- Understanding the Unchurched
- Campus Impact Plan
- Programming with a Purpose

I have read the above and accept the *Student Impact Team* commitment.

Student Signature   _____

Parent Signature   _____

Date   _____

Sample

MINISTRY AREA CHOICES

THURSDAY NIGHT LEADERSHIP TEAM

Duties

- Assist in administering weekly programs
  - √ Advertising (making flyers, developing incentives to bring friends, etc.)
  - √ Programming
  - √ Regular location scouting
- Work closely with admin team developing a student list
- Contact students
- Help in youth-office administration

Skills/Gifts That Will Be Developed

- Administration
- Computer skills
- Up-front leadership
- Interpersonal skills for contacting students

OUTREACH TEAM

Duties

- Work with admin team researching the unchurched student
- Plan monthly outreaches focusing on reaching those who aren't coming to church
  - √ Advertising (making flyers, developing incentives to bring friends, etc.)
  - √ Programming
  - √ Getting dynamic speakers who are familiar with unchurched crowds
- Organize mission trips

√ Local (inner-city, convalescent homes)
√ Uttermost parts (the Mexico trip, Cornerstone, LA World Impact inner-city outreach, etc.)
- Help in youth-office administration

Skills/Gifts That Will Be Developed
- Administration
- Computer skills
- Compassion

CONTACT TEAM

Duties
- Work hand in hand with admin team keeping student databases current
- Contact first-time students each week after attending
- Contact students who attend church and invite them to youth group
- Contact students who have missed four weeks in a row and tell them they're missed
- Contact students who sign up for certain events, etc., to provide information
- Develop/manage e-mail database

Skills/Gifts That Will Be Developed
- Administration
- Computer skills
- Interpersonal skills (contacting students)

SPECIAL EVENTS TEAM

Duties
- Assist in planning annual calendar
- Plan monthly events
  √ Advertising (making flyers, developing incentives to bring friends, etc.)
  √ Programming

√ Getting dynamic speakers
- Work closely with outreach team on events
- Contact students
- Help in youth-office administration

Skills/Gifts That Will Be Developed
- Administration
- Computer skills
- Up-front leadership
- Interpersonal skills (contacting students)

DRAMA TEAM

Duties
- Find/write, practice and perform weekly dramas for Thursday night
- Develop street dramas for outreach, coordinating with outreach team
- Work on year-end play at church

Skills/Gifts That Will Be Developed
- Acting
- Art/set dressing
- Up-front leadership

JUNIOR HIGH STAFF TEAM

Duties
- Attend weekly junior high night and staff meeting
- Assist in planning monthly events
  - √ Advertising (making flyers, developing incentives to bring friends, etc.)
  - √ Programming
  - √ Get dynamic speakers
- Mentor students
- Contact students
- Help in junior high youth-office administration

Skills/Gifts That Will Be Developed

- Patience
- Compassion
- Administration
- Computer skills
- Up-front leadership
- Interpersonal skills (contacting students)

ADMIN TEAM

Duties

- Assist all teams with their database needs
- Make flyers as needed for programs events
- Take Impact minutes and distribute to team
- Help in youth-office administration
- Lay out monthly newsletter
- Write and send weekly e-mail newsletter

Skills/Gifts That Will Be Developed

- Administration
- Computer skills
- Writing
- Teamwork

Sample

WILL YOU BE MY MENTOR?

As a student leader for Community Church, I need to meet weekly with a Christian adult mentor. Would you consider being my mentor? A mentor is a caring adult who is willing to meet with a student weekly, talk about weekly highs and lows, and study through a book or discipleship guide. All discipleship materials will be provided.

Student Name _____

Please fill out the following basic information:

Mentor Name _____
Address _____
Phone(s) _____ E-mail _____
Have you ever discipled/mentored someone before? ❑ Yes ❑ No
If yes, please give details. _____
_____

If needed, would you be willing to meet with 2 students in one meeting?
❑ Yes ❑ No
When would you be available to meet? _____

 1. Please share when and how you became a Christian.

 2. Please share what you are doing to continue to grow in your faith in Christ.

As you can see from these sample forms, we didn't let just any student with a pulse join our staff team. I was looking for students who wanted to make a difference and were willing to make an investment of time. You may choose to be a little more flexible (or a little more rigid).

As you can also see, we had many different teams using different students with different gifts. They all took part in the training and leadership development, but then they divided into different teams and worked on their areas of leadership with a staff person. I assigned a staff person to each ministry area to help provide vision and guidance.

The last team that I put together like this had about 25 student leaders. They were all trained in evangelism and programming. It was great to have student leaders who understood the purpose and were actively taking a part in making it happen.

CHOOSING YOUR TEAM

After students turn in applications, a filtering process needs to occur. I do this by first reviewing the applications with some of my staff and then setting up interviews with the students. These interviews are good opportunities to hear the students' hearts and listen for the areas in which they might be interested in working. These interviews will also help you screen out students who shouldn't be leaders.

Usually, a good application filters out a lot of the students who shouldn't be applying—truthfully some students just won't meet the requirement of living "a lifestyle befitting one who is a role model and an ambassador of Christ." For example, I had a student who showed great leadership skills. Other students in the church loved him, he was popular on campus and he was great up front. Yet this kid couldn't keep his mouth shut. There wasn't an event that went by at which he wasn't getting in a fight, mouthing off to staff or just plain disrupting the event. Bottom line, he didn't live the lifestyle required to be an effective ambassador for Christ.

I hate turning a student away who wants to be on the team. That's why I set up such a stringent application and interview process. Any student who takes the time to fill out the application and secure a weekly mentor and is willing to commit the time is basically in. But every once in a while you'll interview a student who simply shouldn't be on the team. Use this as an opportunity to talk with that student about the problem and lay out a plan to work on it with an end goal of joining the team. This can work as incredible motivation for life change in students.

MINISTRY AREAS/LEADERSHIP ROLES

As you can see in our application package, there are many different ministry areas to which students can choose to apply themselves in a student leadership program. One student could help administer outreach programs, while another maintains the student database. Creating such a variety of ministry jobs or leadership roles may seem cumbersome to plan or maintain, but the reward is well worth it.

If you want to see a brother or sister in Christ blossom, find their gifts and enable them to use them. There is no greater joy than being used by God in the area of your strength. Now this isn't a chapter on spiritual gifts, and it would take too long to teach that in this chapter, but I recommend using some method to discover students' gifts and strengths so they can use those in your ministry. Here are some possible leadership roles:

- Teaching Bible studies
- Leading a small group
- Calling new students each week
- Drama teams
- Organizing activities, trips and programs
- Doing sound or video
- Designing/producing flyers/newsletters
- Singing or playing in the worship team

Some youth workers give a spiritual-gifts test that asks student leaders questions about what they enjoy and where they've been used by God in the past. Other youth workers may just include questions in the interview process. There is no single all-powerful method. Just make sure that you don't just assign a student to do announcements each week when they really want to be used behind the scenes. Take the time to find out what each student's area of strength is and place them in that area.

I worked in a student leadership program once in which we brought in a guy who gave every student leader a spiritual-gifts test. That year we had students with a passion to teach leading Bible studies and sharing in front of the whole group. We had people with the gift of compassion running mission-outreach programs and planning day trips to nursing homes and homeless shelters. It was incredible to see God using people in the areas of their gifts.

The possibilities are endless. Just plan a time, either during the interview process or on the retreat, simply to *listen* to the student leader. Find out what their gifts are and help them use those gifts for Christ.

LEADERSHIP RETREAT

Once we have our team together, we kick off the year with a student leadership retreat exclusively for student leaders and staff. This is a great way to begin, and I use this time to lay the groundwork for the ministry we'll be doing throughout the upcoming year.

The temptation is to try to immediately train students to plan good programs, lead good games and run fantastic activities and events. After all, these are important skills. But let's look back at what Jesus modeled for us. Early in His ministry, He taught His disciples the basics in Matthew 5—7 in the Sermon on the Mount. In this sermon, Jesus taught that money, status and power aren't important. Instead, He upheld models of things like righteousness, meekness, humility and compassion.

Start off the year by teaching student leaders about relying on Christ and developing integrity and personal character. Build this foundation with your student leaders so that they can build a ministry on the only foundation that lasts: a relationship with Christ.

I also like these retreats to be a time of team building. I include team-building exercises that might be as simple as stringing a rope about five feet off the ground between two trees. Then I tell the team to get everyone over the rope, pretending it's an electric fence. I don't give any other instructions. The group has to work together to get one person over and then start passing everyone else over until finally one student will have to make a flying leap into everyone else's arms.

A leadership retreat is also a great time to get student leaders used to their individual ministry areas. I divide them into ministry areas with their assigned staff person several times throughout the weekend to discuss a given topic or to start planning or working on upcoming projects. Each ministry group starts bonding together and gets excited about their ministry area.

On the next couple of pages, you'll find an outline of a student leadership retreat that I helped with a few years back.

Sample Agenda

STUDENT IMPACT TEAM
LEADERSHIP RETREAT AGENDA

FRIDAY

9:00 A.M.	Leave from youth office
11:00 P.M.	Arrive at cabin, unload, get settled, assign K.P.
12:00 P.M.	Lunch
1:00 P.M.	Gather together for Program 1

Program 1

- Gather together
- Circle up, give name and possible ministry area
- The Heart Behind Impact
- Share agenda and logistics for weekend
- Getting into the Word, a time alone in the Bible

—Break—

- Teamwork exercise or game
- Prayer time
- Christian character
- Character wrap-up

3:00 P.M.	Free time
5:00 P.M.	Dinner crew, cook
5:30 P.M.	Dinner
6:30 P.M.	Gather together for Program 2

Program 2

- Teamwork exercise or game
- Prayer time
- "Above Reproach" and what that means
- "Above Reproach Sacrifices" wrap-up

- A time alone with God

—Break—

- Programs That Reach Different Kids
- Break into ministry areas and discuss how it applies to area

8:30 P.M.	Free time for board games, snacks, snipe hunting, etc.
11:00 P.M.	Taco Bell run!
12:00 A.M.	Lights out

Good Night!

SATURDAY

8:00 A.M.	Breakfast
9:00 A.M.	Gather together for Program 3

Program 3

- Crowd breaker
- Prayer time
- Input discussion on friends, media and mind
- "The Vine and the Branches" exercise
- "Connected to the Source" (John 15)

—Break—

- Gather together for "Making a Difference"
- Meet in ministry areas and plan

11:45 A.M.	Lunch preparation
12:00 P.M.	Lunch
12:45 P.M.	A time with God
1:00 P.M.	Send-off

Clean Up and Leave!

REGULAR MEETINGS/TRAINING

Regular student leadership meetings are essential to a student leadership team. After a retreat, there needs to be a regular time that the team gets together as a student leadership team to be refreshed, challenged and better equipped to do ministry.

There are so many powerful principles and tools we can teach students. The trick is finding the balance. Use your regular time together wisely. Allow time for getting to know each other, praying and encouraging; then have small bite-sized training activities that students can pull from and use that week.

Allow time for the individual ministry areas to get together. Many of these individual teams get together more often than just the time you provide. But it is still important to provide that regular time as a minimum. This gets students used to working together and excites them about projects in process. Hold students accountable to this time to accomplish ministry goals and tasks.

IT'S WORTH IT!

As you can see, a student leadership program can really help a youth group. Student leaders help the youth workers get necessary tasks done. These leaders also feel the incredible joy of being used by God to make a difference in the lives of other students. Those fringe students will see fellow students shining for Christ with their actions and service. Regular attendees will hear about the fun retreats and weekly sessions that the leaders take part in, and they will want to become student leaders themselves.

Student leadership takes a lot of work, but the reward is worth it. Follow Jesus' example: develop the Thousands, the Hundred and—don't forget—the Twelve.

A Simple Gospel Presentation

I have often referred to a gospel presentation in this book. The phrase "a gospel presentation" is used rather loosely, so I thought it would be important to communicate to you how to present the good news, the gospel, the story of how Jesus saved us. It is extremely important to be ready at any given moment to share Jesus' story simply, clearly and memorably.

Is there a certain tract, tool or method we should use when presenting the gospel? Good question. I'm not going to teach you one single specific way in which to present it. I'm going lay out the gospel. Nearly any tract or other tool can be used to follow it.

Stories and personal examples are also very important in illustrating the gospel.

OOPS! I DID IT AGAIN!

I remember a time when I royally messed up a chance to share about my relationship with God with a friend I was working with in sales. He and I were in the car on an hour-long drive. He knew my beliefs and had asked me questions every once in a while, usually about church or why he shouldn't sleep with his girlfriend. This particular day he asked me point-blank, "So what is it that you actually believe about God?"

Let's face it, this cuts down to the nitty-gritty. All I had to do was clearly explain the gospel to this guy. Here's where we need to ask ourselves: *Is a canned presentation adequate in this type of situation?*

Well, I didn't have a canned presentation. As a matter of fact, I panicked and didn't know what direction to go in, so I started rambling about how the Bible was accurate and that archeology supported creationism. Within two minutes I created more questions in his mind than he had when he approached me. Again, I had proved to myself that I desperately needed to be able to explain to someone what God had done for me.

Most of us who have been saved by grace and have put our trust in Him remember the details of what happened. And regardless of our background, the same thing happened in each one of us. Each of us tried to live life *our way* instead of *His way*. This separated us from any relationship with Him. We came to a point at which we knew we couldn't go any further and knew we needed a Savior. We became aware of the fact that Jesus paid the price for everything we have ever done wrong and *only He* could save us from our separation from God. We asked Him to forgive our sins and take over our lives. Now we live our life by daily putting our trust in Him.

That is every Christian's testimony. The problem is that many of us just don't know how to express it. So how can we express it?

FOUR FACTS IN THE BIBLE THAT YOU SHOULDN'T MISS!

Here are four biblical facts that you can share with someone about a relationship with God. Getting to this point could take some time. I don't recommend going up to people and saying, "Hi, my name is Mary. You're going to hell, so I need to share the gospel with you." But we must be intentional about building relationships and looking for open doors. When opportunities come up, we need to know what to share.

If I have an opportunity to share the gospel, I share the following four points—without exception. I might adjust the illustrations, the length of the presentation, the wording; or I might tell my own story, but I always include these four simple points because they *are* the gospel!

POINT ONE: GOD'S LOVE

> For by him all things were created (Colossians 1:16).

God loves you and created you to have a personal relationship with Him. You may remember a commercial that started like a scene from the movie *Armageddon*. Huge fireballs plummeted to Earth, destroying buildings, landscapes and wildlife. The scene shifts to heaven where God is pouring Tabasco sauce on something and missing the bowl entirely. As the scene shifts back to Earth, we realize that these fireballs are God's drops of Tabasco that He is carelessly sprinkling on His sandwich, missing the sandwich entirely and hitting Earth.

Just like virtually all commercials or movies that portray God, this commercial portrays Him with a long white beard and wearing a long white robe. This commercial also proposes that God makes stupid mistakes. Other representations of God commonly portray Him as judgmental, mean, spiteful and *definitely* not fun to be around.

Most Americans have a common perception of God. They either think of Him as this uncaring old guy with the beard and the robe, or as some far-out intangible impersonal and unreachable being.

When presenting the gospel and communicating that God loves us and wants a relationship with us, we need to recognize that these misconceptions exist. Most people today don't know that God wants a relationship with them. They don't know that He wants us to call Him Daddy. They don't know that He is willing to forgive our entire past if we would just come home to Him.

The best way to communicate this to someone is by telling them the story of the prodigal son from Luke 15:11-32. If I have the time, I tell that story; if not, I just clarify who God is in a nutshell.

In a Nutshell: Unlike what some may think, God isn't just some old prune with a long white beard who is waiting to bonk us over the head with a Bible every time we step out of line. He loves us and created us with the intention of our having a personal relationship with Him.

POINT TWO: THE BARRIER

> For all have sinned and fall short of the glory of God (Romans 3:23).

Our sin keeps us from having a personal relationship with God. Even though God wants a relationship with us, all of us have messed up that relationship with our sin. Be sure to clarify that sin is simply my running things my way instead of God's way. Don't just throw around the word "sin" and expect everyone to actually understand what it means.

> **In a Nutshell:** Romans 3:23 tells us that "all have sinned." What does the word "all" mean to you? Does it include those people sitting over there? Does "all" include the current teen heart-throbs? Does "all" include the Pope? Does "all" include me? Does "all" include *you*? Yes, yes, yes, yes and *yes*! So all of us are in the same boat no matter how good or bad we are!

POINT THREE: THE ANSWER

> Jesus answered, "I am the way and the truth and the life. No one comes to the Father except through me" (John 14:6).

Only through Jesus Christ can you have a personal relationship with God. The good news is that Jesus is the answer to our broken relationship with God. Jesus is the only way to restore the barrier in our relationship with God. Are you sure that John 14:6 doesn't say "No one comes to the Father except through Buddha?" Are you sure it doesn't say "No one comes to the Father except through belief in a crystal and their inner self?" Are you sure it doesn't say "No one comes to the Father except those who go to church, help old ladies across the street and give money to the Salvation Army?" Are you sure it doesn't say "No one comes to the Father except through any of the many ways you can get there?" It says Jesus is the *only* way.

> **In a Nutshell:** The Bible says that Jesus is the *only* way to the Father—to a relationship with God. Even going to church or doing good deeds isn't enough; only in accepting what Jesus freely offers—salvation—will you ever have a restored relationship with God.

A Must-Tell Story

Share the scenario of driving in your brand-new red Camaro (see p. 107). It's a great visual segue into the real-life fact that Jesus really did come down from His position as judge to be our Savior. He paid the price for our sins by dying on the cross. Every sin you ever committed and *will* commit was paid for on the Cross. Christ rose again that we may live in a relationship with Him forever. All you have to do is respond.

POINT FOUR: THE RESPONSE

> For God so loved the world that he gave his one and only Son, that whoever believes in him shall not perish but have eternal life (John 3:16).

You must personally respond by trusting Jesus Christ as Savior and Lord. All of these facts mean nothing without point four. Sure, it's cool that God created us for a relationship with him. Sure, man separated himself from God by sinning. And it's cool that Jesus paid that price for us. But so what? All of that means nothing if we don't do anything about it.

> **In a Nutshell:** The Bible says very clearly that if we believe in Jesus Christ, we won't perish. I don't know about you, but I want to know what "believe" means here in this verse; because if I do believe, I won't perish. If I do trust in Him, I can have a relationship with Him. I want more than to simply say I believe; I want to have a relationship with Christ and let Him change my heart!

A Must-Tell Story

Share the real-life story of the Great Blondin (see p. 103). This is a wonderful example of the difference between saying you believe and actually believing.

THE CHOICE

All of this information places each of us in one of three categories. Each one of us is either:

1. Someone who has already put their faith in Jesus and asked Him to forgive their sins and run their life;
2. Someone who wants to ask Jesus to forgive them and to have a relationship with them; or
3. Someone who does not want a relationship with God.

Here is where you get down to the nitty-gritty. You have just explained the road to salvation: the relationship we're suppose to have, the barrier of sin, the conquering of sin by Jesus and the step of faith we must make. Now it's time to ask the person you're talking with to reveal whether or not they have a relationship with God. This is difficult for some students because they don't use the biblical facts they just learned to make this judgment; instead they use logic or feelings to explain why they are or are not saved.

Regardless of the choice they make, go back to the definitions of a relationship with God (all four steps) and ask them if they indeed fall into that category according to those facts. For example, Tonya chooses choice 1, saying "I have a personal relationship with God." You simply review steps 1, 2, 3 and 4 and ask "So you understood that God wanted a relationship with you, but sin was in the way? Jesus however paid the price for those sins, and so you responded to Him at a specific time and asked Him to forgive your sins and you began to trust Him to direct your life?" If she says yes, you simply reply "Oh, that's great. When did you make that decision?" This helps you to make sure that the student you are talking with has really made the commitment they claim they have. If they reveal that they don't have a relationship with Christ, simply ask the question, "Would you like to?"

PRAYING FOR SALVATION

If they decide that they would like a personal relationship with Jesus, pray with them right then and there. Tell them that you will pray first; then they will. Review with them the following prayer that summarizes the four main points:

> Dear Father, I am separated from a relationship with God and nothing I do can restore that. I need You in my life, Lord. Jesus, forgive me for my sins. Thank You for paying the penalty for me.
>
> Jesus, I realize that I can't run my life my own way. Please run my life for me. I don't want to just say that I believe, Lord, I want to live out that belief.

Pray first, thanking God for this person. Then thank God that the person is going to pray the following steps (repeat again what they will pray).

Encourage them to pray. If you need to, help them remember; however, it's best to let them pray in their own words so that you know they understand it.

After they pray, affirm to them that their trust in Jesus Christ begins a lifelong relationship with Him.

A MUST-TELL STORY

Share this scenario:

> My friend said that the best day of his life was his wedding day. His wife looked beautiful, he was all spiffed out in a tux, and all of their friends were there. So they walked down the aisle, said their vows and kissed. Then they each went out a separate door and never saw each other again. No, wait! That's not what happened. They left together and lived in the same house.

Make the point that when you truly have a relationship with God, He lives with you.

DON'T FORGET!

The person who just received Christ should receive some affirmation for their decision. Call or take the person to a Christian friend and have them tell your Christian friend what decision they just made. Hopefully, they will receive a hug and a "Welcome to the family of God!" This will do two things: It will make them verbalize what they just did (a lot like them praying the prayer by themselves), and it will make them feel encouraged in the decision they just made. It is good to do this several times with several different Christian friends.

These reproducible pages are placed here for your convenience. If you would like to have full-page versions, you can go to thesourcefym.com and print them out for use in your youth-group meetings and events.

If you choose to copy any of the following pages, please use these guidelines:

HOW TO MAKE CLEAN COPIES FROM THIS BOOK

You may make copies of portions of this book with a clean conscience if
- you (or someone in your organization) are the original purchaser;
- you are using the copies you make for a noncommercial purpose (such as teaching or promoting your ministry) within your church or organization;
- you follow the instructions provided in this book.

However, it is illegal for you to make copies if
- you are using the material to promote, advertise or sell a product or service other than for your ministry fund-raising;
- you are using the material in or on a product for sale; or
- you or your organization are not the original purchaser of this book.

By following these guidelines you help us keep our products affordable. Thank you,
Gospel Light

Permission to make photocopies of or to reproduce by any other mechanical or electronic means in whole or in part any designated* page, illustration or activity in this book is granted only to the original purchaser and is intended for noncommercial use within a church or other Christian organization. None of the material in this book may be reproduced for any commercial promotion, advertising or sale of a product or service. Sharing of the material in this book with other churches or organizations not owned or controlled by the original purchaser is also prohibited. All rights reserved.

*Pages with the following notation can be legally reproduced:

BASIC INFO CARD

Today's Date _____

Your Name _____

Address _____

Phone _____

E-mail _____

School _____

Grade _____

Birth Date _____

Parent/Guardian's Name _____

Our Future in Question

GOAL SHEET—WHERE I WANT TO BE IN THE FUTURE

WHERE I'LL BE IN 5 YEARS

My age _____   My marital status _____
Where I'll be living _____
My occupation or course of study, if still a student _____
My income _____
What my life will be like _____
_____

WHERE I'LL BE IN 10 YEARS

My age _____   My marital status _____
Where I'll be living _____
My occupation or course of study, if still a student _____
My income _____
What my life will be like _____
_____

WHERE I'LL BE IN 20 YEARS

My age _____   My marital status _____
Where I'll be living _____
My occupation _____
My income _____
What my life will be like _____
_____

What's the Deal with Sex?

THINK ABOUT IT

1. In what ways do girls manipulate guys?

2. In what ways do guys manipulate girls?

3. What do girls really want in a relationship with a guy? Do they want sex, or are they looking for something else?

4. What do guys want in a relationship? Does a guy expect the same or more from his girlfriend or wife?

5. Movies, society and condom companies today say that sex is a leisure activity that you should enjoy. What are the consequences of having sex before marriage?

6. Summarize each of the following verses in one sentence:

Flee from sexual immorality. All other sins a man commits are outside his body, but he who sins sexually sins against his own body. Do you not know that your body is a temple of the Holy Spirit, who is in you, whom you have received from God? You are not your own; you were bought at a price. Therefore honor God with your body (1 Corinthians 6:18-20).

It is God's will that you should be sanctified: that you should avoid sexual immorality; that each of you should learn to control his own body in a way that is holy and honorable, not in passionate lust like the heathen, who do not know God; and that in this matter no one should wrong his brother or take advantage of him. The Lord will punish men for all such sins, as we have already told you and warned you. For God did not call us to be impure, but to live a holy life. Therefore, he who rejects this instruction does not reject man but God, who gives you his Holy Spirit (1 Thessalonians 4:3-8).

7. The Bible is clear that premarital sex is wrong. Is that hard to hear? Why or why not?

8. Do the clothes that girls wear affect guys? If so, what should we do about this?

9. Sometimes, even if people make the decision to wait for sex until marriage, they still fail. Very often they'll say things like: "It was just too difficult!" "It was like trying to put out a raging fire!" What situations should we avoid that might bring us to this point of no return?

10. Where is the line of how far you'll go? How can you keep from crossing over that line?

Happy Valentine's Day

IT WAS *NOTHING!*

CAST

The groom, John, wearing a bow tie

The bride, Anna, wearing a veil

The five other women: Christy, Jennifer, Trixie, Los Angeles girl, Roxanne

The preacher, holding a Bible

SCENE

The scene opens with John and Anna holding hands and standing in front of the preacher, partway through their wedding ceremony. Suddenly another girl comes forward and crowds in between the happy couple, grabbing John's hand too.

Anna: (*Whispering to John.*) What's going on?!?

John: (*Whispers back.*) Oh, Hon, ignore her—she's nothing!

Anna: (*Whispering a little louder.*) What do you mean "Ignore her"? How can I ignore her? She's up here standing between us!

John: (*Trying to move the preacher along.*) Anna, trust me. Her name is Christy. She doesn't mean anything to me. She's from the past. It's totally over between us.

Anna: (*Still trying to whisper.*) Well, what was it *then*—you know, in the past?

John: (*Shrugs shoulders.*) We thought we had something special then; that's why we . . . but . . . anyway, that was a long time ago and—

Anna: (*Loudly.*) You *slept* with her?

John: (*Pleading, trying to talk low.*) Anna, that was a long time ago; I love only you now. Don't you love me?

Anna: (*Angrily.*) This isn't the way I planned this day.

Another girl walks up, crowds in and holds hands as well.

Anna: (*Turns to John.*) And who is *this*?

John: (*Uncomfortable.*) I can't remember her name. (*Pause.*) Jennifer, I think. She's just a girl I met at a party.

Anna: I assume you are going to tell me she means nothing either?

John: Yeah! Honey, it meant nothing.

Anna: (*Trying to whisper but getting angrier.*) "It"?!? What is "it"? You mean you slept with her too?

John: (*Trying to calm his bride-to-be.*) Anna, we don't need to go through my entire past right now.

Anna: (*Hands on hips.*) Yeah, well the subject seems to keep coming up!

John: Anna, I love only you.

Another two girls come up, squeeze in and hold hands with the group.

Anna: (*Fuming.*) All right John! Who are *they*?

John: (*Frustrated.*) They're nothing, Honey, really! I can't even remember their names.

Anna: And this is supposed to make me happy? How do I know that I'm not just some girl whose name you'll forget?

John: That won't ever happen, Anna, I love *you* now. Not Christy, Jennifer, Trixie or—what was her name—oh, well, the weekend-in-Los-Angeles girl.

Anna: What weekend?

John: You don't want to know.

Anna: I just thought that you and I would have this special thing together.

John: It *will* be special!

Another girl walks up, smiling.

John: Roxanne?

Anna runs out crying and John chases after.

AMISTAD

Have each group member finish the following statements in turn:

1. When I think of the Bible, I think of . . .
2. When I think of God, I think of . . .
3. When I think of Jesus, I think of . . .

WHAT DO YOU KNOW ABOUT JESUS?

1. Who was Jesus?

2. When did He live?

3. What was He famous for?

4. Was He a real person, and how can we know for sure?

5. Do you think His life has any meaning for us today?

True or False?

Write *T* for true or *F* for false for each statement; then answer the questions that follow. After everyone has completed the questions, go around the circle for everyone's answers. (Turn this sheet upside down for the correct answers to the true/false questions.)

_____ Jesus claimed to be able to forgive sins.

_____ Jesus claimed to be the Son of God.

_____ Jesus existed as God before His birth.

_____ Jesus claimed to be God in human flesh.

_____ Jesus claimed that He would come back to life after He was killed.

_____ Jesus claimed that He could grant eternal life.

_____ Jesus claimed that He is the only way to have a relationship with God.

_____ Jesus claimed that He is the only way to heaven.

1. Which of these claims is hardest to believe?

2. Which of these is easiest to believe?

3. Which of these claims surprises you the most?

ANSWER: ALL ARE TRUE.

BABE: PIG IN THE CITY

1. What do you think Babe thought of the pit bull the whole time he was being chased by it?

2. Why did Babe have mercy on the pit bull? What benefit was there in doing this?

3. What benefit is there in getting revenge instead?

4. Share a situation in which you had an opportunity to show kindness to an enemy.

THE EMPIRE STRIKES BACK

1. In John 3:16, John used the word "believe." What does that really mean?

2. What are some areas in our lives that might demonstrate a lack of belief?

3. If we put our trust in God in that area of our life, would He come through? How? (Remember Luke's line, "I don't believe it," and Yoda's response, "That is why you failed.")

FORREST GUMP

1. Does God listen to all our prayers? Why?

2. Does God answer all our prayers? Why?

3. Why doesn't God answer our prayers in the way we want them answered?

4. How do difficult times (like the storm) make you feel toward God?

5. Why can't we predict or understand God's plans for us?

6. Has there been a time when circumstances in your life were bad, but God used them for good?

GHOST

1. Why do people fear death?

2. How can a person prepare to die?

3. Is death the end of the road? What else is there?

4. Who do you think heaven is for? How do you get there?

5. Who do you think hell is for? How do you get there?

A SIMPLE PLAN

1. What would you do if you found a bag filled with millions of dollars?

2. What if you had to lie to keep it?

3. What if you had to kill someone to keep it?

4. Can money make people happy? Why or why not?

5. Everyone in the movie was happier before they found the money than after they found it. Why is that?

6. Can you think of a time that you really wanted something and then you finally got it? What was that like? Did your whole life change for the better once you got what you wanted?

DISPOSABLE CAMERA RALLY

MANDATORY PICTURES

Must have pictures of all of the following to qualify:

- ❑ The entire team making faces at the camera
- ❑ Two team members eating the same piece of licorice
- ❑ Someone in the group lying down in a bed
- ❑ The entire team standing on their heads

1,000 POINT PICTURES

- ❑ A team member feeding a stranger
- ❑ A lady holding a child's hand
- ❑ A guy smoking
- ❑ A gas station attendant washing a window
- ❑ A couple on a park bench
- ❑ Someone ordering Chinese food
- ❑ A lady walking her dog

1,500 POINT PICTURES

- ❑ A person driving a bus
- ❑ A firefighter in uniform
- ❑ A team member combing someone's hair
- ❑ Someone buying dog food
- ❑ A little kid licking a sucker
- ❑ Someone preaching on a street corner
- ❑ A team member hugging a car salesman

3,000 POINT PICTURES

- ❑ A dog relieving itself
- ❑ A couple on a bicycle built for two
- ❑ A team member helping an elderly person across the street
- ❑ A police car with its lights flashing
- ❑ Someone walking past a sign that says something like "Do Not Enter" or "Do Not Pass"
- ❑ The entire team on a boat

MANHUNT

Find a high school student

❏ With red hair

❏ With a 4.0 GPA

❏ Who is on the football team

❏ With a tattoo

❏ Who drives a Honda

❏ Who took geometry in ninth grade

❏ Who smells really good

❏ Who plays on the volleyball team

❏ Who is a cheerleader

❏ Who dyes their hair

❏ Who can belch their name

MEMOREX MADNESS

Record the following sounds:

❏ A baby crying

❏ A toilet flushing

❏ A siren

❏ A burp

❏ A lion's roar

❏ Someone singing out of tune

❏ A jet taking off

❏ A Kmart intercom announcement

❏ A used-car commercial

❏ Someone arguing

❏ A church organ

❏ Someone swimming

❏ A dog barking

Video Scavenger Hunt

Note: All videotaped items must be filmed in enough light in order to be clearly seen!

Mandatory Items

Must have all of the following to qualify:

❑ A creative introduction to your team's video
❑ Three team members being pushed in a shopping cart
❑ A team member spontaneously interviewing three strangers, asking, "What is your conception of God?" or "What is God like?"
❑ A team member chugging an entire can of Pepsi and belching
❑ The whole team hanging upside down while singing "The Pledge of Allegiance" to the tune of the theme from *Gilligan's Island*

1,000 Point Items

❑ A team member hugging a stranger
❑ A lady scolding a child
❑ A guy coming out of the girl's bathroom
❑ A grocery clerk singing a recognizable song
❑ Two teenagers kissing
❑ Someone ordering a cheeseburger without any cheese
❑ A lady walking a dog
❑ Your entire team on one tree

1,500 Point Items

❑ Someone peeling out in a car (team vehicles not included)
❑ A firefighter in uniform
❑ Someone (other than a team member) buying Depends undergarments
❑ Someone making a citizen's arrest
❑ A little kid singing "Mary Had a Little Lamb"
❑ Someone giving a stranger a noogie
❑ A team member hugging a gas station attendant

3,000 Point Items

❑ A dog relieving itself on a fire hydrant

❑ A traffic accident

❑ Your entire team waist deep in water

❑ A police car (other than the one at the traffic accident) with its siren on (not its lights—its siren)

❑ Someone crawling out of a manhole

❑ Your entire team coming out of a VW Bug

25,000 Point Item

❑ A 300-pound Rottweiler eating an entire Carl's Jr. salad bar

500,000 Point Item

❑ The entire team hovering over a major league baseball field, balancing a stack of seven baseballs on their noses and reciting *Hamlet* backward

JONATHAN'S MINISTRY PLANNING CHECKLIST

HOW WELL DO I PLAN AHEAD?

> **Note:** This quiz is designed for a church youth ministry. If your ministry is a specialized ministry (e.g., a campus outreach ministry, a student leadership ministry, etc.), then certain questions will not apply to your ministry.

Circle *Y* for yes and *N* for no in each of the following questions. If you are ever doubtful of an answer, circle the answer on the right (whether it be *Y* or *N*) for that question.

Start with a purpose.

1. Y/N   Do we have a purpose, vision or mission statement?
2. Y/N   Do we consider this statement when we plan programs and events?

List all the events, activities and programs possible.

1. Y/N   Do we consider and/or look for new events, activities and programs for our ministry?
2. Y/N   Have we ever brainstormed new ideas with staff members or students?
3. Y/N   Have we ever checked out another ministry to get programming ideas?

Match events, activities and programs to your purposes.

1. Y/N   Do we ever plan a single event, activity or program in which we try to reach ALL types of students at that event?
2. Y/N   Do we plan events, activities or programs in which we target or try to reach out to unchurched students?
3. Y/N   Did we ever give a gospel invitation last year at an outreach event?
4. Y/N   Did we ever bring in a guest speaker for the purpose of outreach/evangelism?

5. Y/N   Do we plan events, activities or programs in which students can grow in their faith?

6. Y/N   Are there Bible studies available for students to plug in to?

7. Y/N   Are there small groups students can plug in to?

8. Y/N   Do students have an opportunity to worship God?

9. Y/N   Do we have a student leadership team?

10. Y/N   Do we plan student leadership events, activities or programs?

11. Y/N   Have we brought in a speaker/trainer to equip students to reach their friends for Christ?

Check your balance.

1. Y/N   Have we evaluated whether or not our events, activities or programs match our purpose?

2. Y/N   Do we have events, activities or programs that are primarily church-kid friendly?

3. Y/N   Do we have events, activities or programs that primarily reach out to students, but don't provide a place of growth?

Start decorating your calendar with your matched events.

1. Y/N   Have we ever made an annual or six-month calendar?

2. Y/N   Do we plan activities and events with enough time to advertise and build up to them?

3. Y/N   Do we have a strategy for attracting students back after visiting an event or program?

4. Y/N   Do we have something planned for new believers *after* a program or event?

5. Y/N   Do we pick up a school calendar to help plan ours?

6. Y/N   Have we checked other neighboring ministries' schedules near us?

7. Y/N   Do we check items of logistical importance—transportation, lodging, staffing—before booking events?

Plan when necessary tasks need to be done.

1. Y/N   Do we use planners, Palm Pilots or some other sort of daily/weekly scheduling/task tools?

2. Y/N   Do we transfer programming to-dos to our scheduling tools?

3. Y/N   Do students know about big events and trips several months out?

4. Y/N   Do we provide fund-raising opportunities months prior to an event or trip?

5. Y/N   Have we booked a speaker, a place of lodging or a vehicle within four weeks of an event this past year?

6. Y/N   Are we tired of these stupid questions?

SCORING

There is no cool mathematical equation that will help you take your score and figure out whether or not you're the next CEO of Youth Specialties. *All* of these questions can individually help us reevaluate and maybe even sharpen certain areas of our ministry.

The answer to each question should be the *Y* or *N* to the left. If you circled the *Y* or *N* to the right, that highlights an area that you should read again and reconsider in your ministry. I don't claim to have all the answers, but I do hope to make us all think about the *why* in many of these areas.

STUDENT LEADERSHIP APPLICATION

Basic Information

Name _____ ❏ Male ❏ Female

Address _____

Phone(s) _____ E-mail _____

Parent/Guardian's Name(s) _____

Grade_____   School _____

Just for Kicks

Favorite thing to do for fun _____

Favorite type of music _____

Favorite movie _____

Your Relationship with God

1. Please share when and how you became a Christian.

2. Please share what you are doing to continue to grow in your faith in Christ.

3. Why do you want to be on the Student Leadership Team?

4. How would your unchurched friends describe your relationship with God?

5. How would your churched friends describe your relationship with God?

6. How would your family describe your relationship with God?

More Great Ways to Reach and Teach Young People

Surviving Adolescence
Learning to Like Yourself and
Making the Right Decisions
Jim Burns
Paperback
ISBN 08307.20650

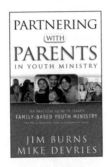

**Partnering with Parents
in Youth Ministry**
The Practical Guide to Today's Family-
Based Youth Ministry—
The Key to Reaching Youth
and Parents for Christ
Jim Burns & Mike DeVries
Paperback
ISBN 08307.32292

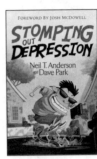

**Stomping Out
Depression**
Overcoming Depression
*Neil Anderson
and Dave Park*
Paperback
ISBN 08307.28929

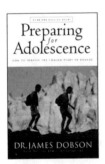

Preparing for Adolescence
Dr. James Dobson
Paperback
ISBN 08307.24974

Family Guide and Workbook
Manual
ISBN 08307.25016

Growth Guide Manual
ISBN 08307.25024

Group Guide
ISBN 08307.25008

**Family Tape Pack—8
Audiocassettes**
ISBN 08307.26357

Family CD Pack—8 CDs
ISBN 08307.31156

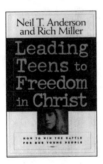

**Leading Teens
to Freedom in Christ**
How to win the battle
for our young people
*Neil T. Anderson
and Rich Miller*
Paperback
ISBN 08307.18400

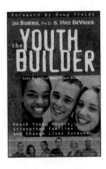

The YouthBuilder
Reaching young people
for Christ and changing
lives forever
*Jim Burns
and Mike DeVries*
Paperback
ISBN 08307.29232

Available at your local Christian bookstore

www.gospellight.com

Gospel Light